CRIMSON NATION

CRIMSON NATION

ELI GOLD

RUTLEDGE HILL PRESS®

Nashville, Tennessee

A Division of Thomas Nelson Publishers
www.thomasnelson.com

Published by Rutledge Hill Press, a Division of Thomas Nelson, Inc., P.O. Box 141000, Nashville,
Tennessee, 37214.

Rutledge Hill Press books may be purchased in bulk for educational, business, fundraising, or sales pro-
motional use. For information, please email SpecialMarkets@ThomasNelson.com.

Library of Congress Cataloging-in-Publication Data

Gold, Eli, 1953–
    Crimson nation / Eli Gold.
      p. cm.
    Includes index.
    ISBN 1-4016-0190-1 (hardcover)
    1. Alabama Crimson Tide (Football team)—History. 2. University of Alabama—Football—
History. I. Title.
    GV958.A4G65 2005
    796.332'63'0976184—dc22
                                                          2005009605

Printed in the United States of America

05 06 07 08 09—5 4 3 2 1

To my personal "Crimson Nation of two"
Claudette and Elise, who love being part of the "Alabama Family"

And to David and Keily Gold who taught their little boy
from Brooklyn how to spread his wings and fly.

Table of Contents

Foreword

FROM THE MOMENT YOU TURN ON A BROADCAST OF AN ALABAMA football game, there is no mistaking whose voice is booming through the radio. As soon as you hear it you know. That's Eli Gold!

My son Johnny, a die-hard Alabama fan, plays the video of the 1992 Year in Review and the highlights of that year's national championship game over and over. When I hear Eli's voice calling the plays of that very special year, I'm immediately transported back to one of the best times of my life as well as a wonderful time in Alabama football history.

When I first came to the University of Alabama as one of Coach Bryant's assistants in 1958, I was thrilled to death. I had worked with him as a student assistant at Texas A&M and to make the move to a great university with a man I loved and respected was as close to perfect as you can get. I was making forty-five hundred dollars a year and thought I had the absolute best job in the world. I loved every minute of it.

To return to the University of Alabama nearly thirty years later as head coach was another thrill for me and my family. Even though I greatly enjoyed the years I spent away from Alabama—many of them working in the NFL—I was happy to be back. There is something very special about coaching college players. When you have a team that clicks, as we did in 1992, everybody comes away from that experience not only as better players and coaches, but as better people.

As far as athletic accomplishments go, winning the national title has to be number one. Not many people get to be part of a national championship team. But as far as real accomplishments are concerned, the most important thing to me was seeing players graduate. I felt I had a responsibility to the mothers and grandmothers I met who told me their son or grandson was the first one in their family to go to college. Seeing them graduate and feel that maybe you had an effect on a player and his life, that was what I really enjoyed.

At Alabama, it was all about relationships. When I was head coach, I was lucky enough to have a great working relationship with Eli Gold, the Voice of the Crimson Tide. Eli was always incredibly professional and great to work with. He was always prepared and on time. We had a great time talking football during those days. Of course, it's easy to have a lot of fun when you are winning so much. What's not fun about that?

I remember many Friday nights and Saturday mornings when my family would get together with Eli's family before we taped our weekly pre-game radio show. Eli earned my confidence quickly and for that reason, I felt comfortable sharing with him the first few plays that we planned to call during the upcoming game. I did this because I wanted him to understand the reason that we planned to run certain plays from certain formations. I hoped this would make it easier for him to explain things to the fans, and I knew he would keep the information to himself until it became time to use it on the air.

I'm pleased to say that Eli and I formed a lasting friendship during those years. During those evenings and mornings together, we spent a lot of time talking about everyday things. I used to enjoy his stories about NASCAR drivers or other sports teams away from football. But of course, most of the time, we talked football and no one talks it better than Eli.

He is a great broadcaster and an extremely talented storyteller. Add that to the fact that he has been an Alabama man for almost two decades and it's easy to see why he is just the guy to write a book of this kind. He knows the game, he knows the team, and Eli is happy to take you behind the scenes into the broadcast booth, down to the field, and way back in history as well.

Eli and I agree that Alabama fans are the most intense, loyal, and dedicated bunch you will ever see. I have often said that in Texas people will talk about a big game like the Texas–Texas A&M matchup for a week or so before and after the game. But in Alabama, football talk is nonstop and year-round. This book is for those fans. I'm proud to count myself among them.

Coach Gene Stallings

A Word From "The Snake"

EVERY FOOTBALL SATURDAY IN TUSCALOOSA WHEN I SIT IN THE press box and look out at the crowd of ninety thousand and it's all crimson and there's that unbelievable excitement of being at an Alabama football game, I always wish that everybody could see what I see. It's hard to explain how special it feels to be up in the booth after having been part of Alabama football as a player and now to broadcast it and talk about it and bring the whole thing to people through radio; it's just incredible.

As the color analyst for the Tide, it's partly my responsibility and great thrill to bring the pageantry and tradition of Alabama football to the fans. Eli Gold, the Voice of the Crimson Tide, who sits next to me during our broadcasts, is really good at painting a picture and delivering it over the radio. He understands that people listening at home can't see what we see. So he paints a picture with words that will help them.

I'm an Xs and Os guy, so I watch a football game with my hands under the center. I try to throw the game at our listeners with a right and a left and an up and a down. Then Eli throws in the wind blowing and the colors and the band playing. The best compliment we get is when someone says, "Thanks for making us be at the game." That's what we shoot for.

For me, talking about football is the most natural thing in the world. The first thing I do every morning is turn on Sports Center. Talking football and trying to figure out how to win is something I've done all my life. It's the only thing I've ever thought about, so when I joined the broadcast team a few years ago, I couldn't have imagined a better job. Coming home felt really good.

There really is something special about Alabama football. I love college football in general. But to play at Alabama, a school that's won twelve championships and dominated the SEC over the years, there's just nothing else like it. The team has such a great tradition, has produced so many great players, and has won so many games—more than anybody! Crimson and white, those colors really resonate with people in this state.

My dad was an Alabama fan. In the late fifties and early sixties, growing up in Foley, Alabama, all I heard my dad talking about was Bama football. We'd listen to games on the radio or read about them in the newspaper. I heard all those names associated with Coach Bryant—Pat Trammel, Billy Neighbors, Billy Richardson. I saw what Alabama football meant to my dad, his friends and the people all around us.

In high school, I was a good athlete. Typical of athletes in small towns, I played just about every sport. I was a good baseball player. I was a pitcher and could throw the ball really hard and had good control. In the early sixties I was offered a chance to play minor-league ball for the Yankees. They offered me fifty thousand dollars, but about the same time, the opportunity came around for me to play football at Alabama. I had to weigh the chance to make some money and throw the baseball against the chance to go and play for Coach Bryant and follow in the footsteps of the great men whose names I'd heard growing up: Pat Trammel, Steve Sloan, and Joe Namath.

Alabama won the national championship in 1961 and in 1964. I wanted to jump in line behind all that. If you're going to play, you want to win championships and Alabama was dominating. So, I went to play for Coach Bryant. Obviously, this turned out to be the best decision of my life.

I've always been free-spirited and independent. At one point, I didn't conform to Coach Bryant's rules, and he suspended me from the team. He knew my wayward ways would cause me to lose out on a great opportunity and he wouldn't let me do that. I was so young and dumb but he figured out a way to grab me by the back of the neck and make me get back in school and make me play. Coach Bryant saved me. There's no doubt about it.

At the Crimson Tide Sports Network, we've got a great team. This time the goal is to put on the best radio broadcast possible. Every one who works on the broadcast does a great job. I love the fact that Eli Gold (a guy from Brooklyn!) can have so much passion for Alabama football! He has the same passion for it that I do. He loves the school and understands the tradition. Eli knows and understands sports. He's great at pulling the human interest part out of every story. We understand each other's role.

We both know the huge responsibility we have to Alabama football fans. I stand out on the quad at the Crimson Village and sign autographs for two hours because I know what Alabama football means to the fans. I look forward to seeing fans and being recognized. I don't mind re-telling the run-in-the-mud-against-Auburn story. It's a compliment. My dad always said, "The time to worry is when no one comes around!"

Everybody who played at Alabama has a common bond. We share a great legacy and now it's time for the new players to establish their legacy. It's time to get back to knowing you're going to a bowl game every year and expecting to win national championships. This attitude has to come from everybody—players, coaches, fans, alumni, the radio broadcast group, all of us! The best way to do that is just go and win. If we do that, then everything works.

Ken Stabler

Acknowledgments

THROUGH THE PAGES OF THIS BOOK, YOU ARE ABOUT TO BEGIN A trip that will, hopefully, bring into the sharpest of focus, the legend that is "The Crimson Tide." Like this famed university and its legendary football program, this book is built upon the shoulders and advice of many.

I am, as you know, an "electronic media" guy. My knowledge of the publishing business is slim at best. That is why I have leaned heavily on "Old IB" MB Roberts, her hugely talented husband and Sports Illustrated photographer Ron Modra, and our esteemed editor, Geoff Stone. They made sure that I avoided all of the land mines and had smooth sailing while getting my first book to print.

The staff at the University of Alabama was, as you can imagine, a true fount of information and guidance. I sincerely appreciate the fact that Dr. Finus Gaston, Larry White, Barry Allen and Wendell Hudson among others, were generous with their time and obliged my occasional request for research and trademark data and general counsel.

As they are on the air, the crew at the Crimson Tide Sports Network were my wingmen on this project. Bert Bank, Tom Stipe, Tom Roberts, Ken Stabler, Butch Owens, Brian Roberts were all a big help. I knew they would be. There is a deep historical well to dip into regarding our favorite university. There is not a better group to count on to "have your back" than those guys and our CTSN boss Michael Alford. True professionals but more importantly all true friends.

I would especially like to thank Larry Black, the producer of the DVD series called *Alabama Football Legends Reunion,* for giving me permission to use quotes from this project. The DVD is a treasure for Alabama fans and is still available at www.sportsreunion.com or by phone at (800) 410-9877.

I must take a moment to acknowledge the greatest fans in the land. The University of Alabama football fans are, bar none, the finest anywhere. The passion with which they support the Tide is unmatched. Period. There were some who questioned me being hired back in 1988. I thank you for giving me the opportunity to grow into this dream job. One can't adequately explain the feeling of being part of the "Alabama Family." It's a feeling of welcome. A feeling of acceptance. A feeling of comfort. I thank you all for allowing me to feel that.

And finally, as the book unfolds, you will realize that many, many people who bleed Crimson and White, took the time to sit for extended interviews. I won't name them all here, but you'll know who they are as the pages flip by. To them I offer a heartfelt thank you. I might be the one telling the story, but you are the people who built this great Crimson Nation.

Enjoy and ROLL TIDE!!!

Introduction

No MATTER WHERE I GO OR WHAT I'M DOING, PEOPLE ALWAYS WANT to talk to me about the Crimson Tide. I guess this shouldn't be much of a surprise since I've been broadcasting Alabama football games for nearly twenty years. Folks know what I do for a living. But it goes beyond my job. People everywhere just want to talk Bama football.

In addition to my duties as play-by-play man for the Tide, I also work for NASCAR's Motor Racing Network (MRN). This job takes me into the pits and garages at NASCAR races. Before each race I visit with drivers and crew chiefs. It never fails: Before I can even ask, "How's the car running this week?" someone will holler out, "What's the Tide got this year?" Sterling Marlin, a big Tennessee fan, always says, "You guys gonna be any good?" Dale Jarrett is a big sports fan. He might say, "Hey, that was some game yesterday." It's a hoot. It doesn't matter what part of the country I'm in. Every day I hear it: "What's the Tide got?" That's just part of being involved with one of the most elite and absolutely unique franchises in existence. No matter what happens—a good year, a bad year—we're still Alabama.

I've always been a sports fan. But as a kid, I didn't follow college football. No one I knew did. I grew up in Brooklyn. We had the Yankees and the Mets, the Giants and the Jets. We also had the Knicks and the Nets plus the Rangers and the Islanders. From the time I was ten years old in 1963 until I left New York in 1976, there was scant little college football televised in New York City. There just weren't any teams anyone cared about. Columbia was something like 0-11 every year. They played in front of about twelve people. Even the players' parents didn't go to the games! Rutgers was not a factor, either. In New York, whenever sports fans grudgingly acknowledged college sports, they talked about St. John's or Notre Dame basketball and the NIT. They never talked about college football. I was a huge sports fan, but I hate to say it, as a kid, I had no idea who Paul "Bear" Bryant was.

When I left New York, I had had enough of the city. It's a magnificent place and I still love going back to visit, but I was tired of the hustle, the bustle, the rudeness, and, frankly, the snobbishness. In Alabama people actually look at you and say, "Good morning." In New York, if a guy nodded at you, it was a courtesy to let you know that a mugger was closing in from the rear.

In the seventies, Marv Albert and his brothers had the New York market tied up very tightly. Mel Allen and Red Barber were doing the Yankees. Lindsey Nelson, Bob Murphy, and Ralph Kiner were doing the Mets. They weren't going anywhere and let's be realistic, I wasn't going to get their jobs even if they did leave. So, in 1976 I moved from New York to Hampton, Virginia, to broadcast games for the American Hockey League team The Hampton Gulls, an affiliate of the Birmingham Bulls. At the time, the Bulls were a member of the World Hockey Association, which had been formed as a rival to the NHL. After a year or so, Bulls' owner John Bassett hired me to be the full-time hockey radio broadcaster in Birmingham. That's what brought me to Alabama.

I loved Birmingham from the start. I loved the slower pace and the far more open spaces. Mostly, I loved the friendliness. At the time, though, I couldn't understand this attraction and obsession with college sports. Why would you want to watch an eighteen-year-old college kid play ball when you could watch a twenty-five-year-old paid professional do it? It took me a little while to understand there was more to life than the pro sports scene. I learned that very quickly. If you live in Alabama, it's impossible not to get caught up in the fervor that is college football.

For twenty-nine years, John Forney served as the legendary Voice of the Crimson Tide. After John left, Paul Kennedy came in for five years. In the spring of 1988, I was on the road when word came that, once his five-year contract expired, Paul Kennedy was not going to be rehired. As a broadcaster you always hate to hear about a guy not being retained.

The next day there were articles in the paper about it. One story included a long list of candidates for the job. The list ended with Eli Gold. The funny thing was, I had never spoken with anybody at Alabama about it. The next day there was another story that said those on the short list were yada yada, yada yada, and Eli Gold. I still hadn't spoken to anybody. Then, on the following Monday a story ran listing the names of those coming in for an interview, and Eli Gold was included. I still hadn't talked to anyone at the university, but I wasn't stupid. I may have been born at night, but it wasn't last night. So, I picked up the phone and called a gentleman at the university, associate athletic director Tommy Limbaugh, the person heading the search for the new Voice of the Tide.

I said, "Mr. Limbaugh, you don't know me. My name is Eli Gold, and according to the newspapers, I'm coming down for an interview." We both had a chuckle, and he said, "Well, would you like to?" The next day I met with him, followed by meetings with basketball coach Wimp Sanderson and football coach Bill Curry. They told me that John Forney, who had initially been replaced by Paul Kennedy, would be coming back to resume his tenure as the Voice of the Tide. John was a wonderful man, truly beloved, and understandably people were ecstatic. The school decided to split the broadcast position between John and me, with John doing football and me basketball.

Courtside smiles with Bama basketball coach Mark Gottfried after another Tide win.

During my first basketball season for the Tide, I also worked at the race-track for MRN on Thursdays and part of Fridays. Then Friday nights I would fly to the Alabama basketball city, whether it was Tuscaloosa or somewhere on the road, and do the game on Saturday. Then after the game I would fly back to the racing city and broadcast the race on Sunday.

One week in February 1989, Tommy Limbaugh called on a Thursday night. He found me at my hotel in Richmond, Virginia, and asked if we could meet the next day in Knoxville at Alabama's basketball practice. I said, sure. Immediately, I was concerned. Why would your boss come all the way to Knoxville to tell you something face-to-face? It was either very bad news— this isn't working out, thank you, see ya, goodbye—or it was something very good. I thought that there was a possibility he was going to offer me the foot-ball job, but I convinced myself it was probably something else.

The next day, I woke up in Richmond, the race city, to a blanket of snow. The airport was closed and I had two big problems: 1) I needed to be in Knoxville for a basketball game the next day and 2) I had agreed to meet Tommy Limbaugh that afternoon at the University of Tennessee's arena. I had to be there!

Due to the snow, my commercial flight was cancelled, but I found a guy

(Left to right): Bert Bank, Tom Roberts, yours truly and Tom Stipe. Just part of The Crimson Tide Sports Network crew.

who knew a pilot. We agreed on a fee, and I hopped into the guy's little private plane. I don't remember if it was a Bonanza, a Piper Cub, or what. We were the first plane off the ground that morning. The runway wasn't even totally cleared yet! A few hours later, I was sitting at midcourt, about sixteen rows up, in the Thompson-Boling Arena with Tommy Limbaugh. After exchanging a few pleasantries, Tommy, with a very resolute look on his face, asked if I would accept the job as the Voice of the Crimson Tide football team. Instantly, I said yes.

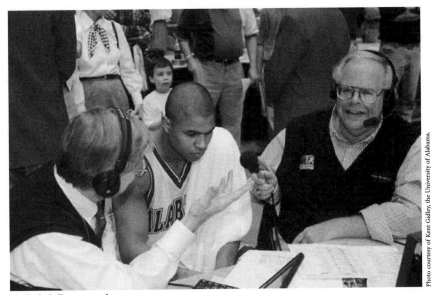

The basketball postgame show.

From the day of the announcement in February until the start of the season in September, the university and I took a lot of heat. Part of the reason for this was the fact that John Forney was beloved in Alabama. Many fans didn't want to see him go, but he had been in ill health, and after he finished his thirtieth year behind the microphones, the administration decided the time was right to make a change. I had lived in Alabama for ten years and had announced Bama basketball for a year, but I was still not perceived as part of "the family." I was known as a pro sports guy. I did NASCAR, pro baseball, pro hockey. To many people, I was simply not an Alabama guy. People wrote to the university and said that if I was hired they would stop contributing money. They wrote that they were taking the university out of their wills. Some people thought my hiring was an absolute disgrace.

I was a young broadcaster who got lucky enough to land one of the most coveted jobs in the nation. But some members of the media tarred and feathered me. I chose to stop listening to sports talk radio at one point. As for the newspapers, there was one guy in particular who complained that I wasn't an Alabama fan because I didn't attend the 1988 Iron Bowl. What he failed to mention, though, was that I was not there because I was out of town broadcasting basketball for the Crimson Tide on November 25, 1988. What should have been the most exciting time instead was a very stressful time. Looking back, I'm glad to say, that time period is now a blip on the radar of the most amazing experience I could have imagined.

Photo courtesy of Kent Gidley, the University of Alabama.

Two great guys with faces for radio. Ken Stabler (left) and Eli.

In 2004 I signed a contract that will take me into my twentieth year, and that makes me enormously happy. I consider myself part of the Alabama family now. There's one reason this job is so rewarding: the incredible, one-of-a-kind fans of Alabama football. You have to be on your toes as a broadcaster here because Alabama fans are walking, talking Crimson Tide encyclopedias! They know their history backward and forward, and they know absolutely everything about University of Alabama athletes.

When I was growing up, my dad and I had Jets season tickets. (I was a huge fan of one Joe Willie Namath, an Alabama-star-turned-Jets-superstar.) I knew the players by name and number, but I sure as heck didn't know if Al Atkinson had a dog and two cats and if his wife's sister's name was Matilda. But Alabama fans know everything about every player, regardless of his status on the depth chart. They'll run up to a first-year, third-string tackle and say, "How are you doing? How's your doggie?" I mean, they know everything. It's wonderful.

How many teams can say they get crowds of forty thousand people in the stadium to watch spring practice games? Bama can. Alabama football is talked about in this state all year long. It's the rallying point.

Football season is an awesome time of year. When the first home game finally arrives, fans paint themselves from head to toe and get busy tailgating like nobody's business. Of course, many fans of college or pro football enjoy tailgating. Plenty of cities boast impressive cookouts and pregame parties. But Alabama fans show up on Tuesday for the game on Saturday. There are 365 days in a year and only seven or eight are designated for Crimson Tide home games. These fans stretch out each of those days as much as possible.

The campus explodes on game day. It's an electric, circuslike atmosphere on the quad where we broadcast our pregame show. There will be Alabama Legends signing autographs in one tent and hospitality booths over here and there's the president greeting everyone. The Million Dollar Band is playing and people are going crazy. Other schools may make their own claims, but Bama *is* the best.

Roll Tide.

ONE

Radio

On the Air

IN 1998 I FOUND OUT THAT MY NEW COLOR MAN WAS GOING TO BE Kenny "the Snake" Stabler. I was excited because of who he is. Who wouldn't be? But I'm a preparation freak. I always go on the air more prepared and with more information than I will ever need. And I expect the same from the other people working on the broadcast. I just didn't know, given Kenny's reputation of being a fun-loving sort of party guy, what we were getting besides a magnificent name.

We can't hide the pride. Eli Gold, The Voice of the Tide and Color Analyst and football legend Ken "The Snake" Stabler.

Photo courtesy of Kent Gidley, the University of Alabama.

9

So, our first game together, I remember thinking, *I hope he shows up and he's prepared.* He is always exceedingly prepared, not only for the game we're doing that day, but for next week's game as well. When we promote the following week's broadcast, Snake's able to give you a nugget or two about something or somebody. He doesn't take the easy route and just say, "Yeah. It's going to be a good game. Anytime Alabama and Arkansas get together . . . ." Snake always has something meaty.

Kenny prepares for a game differently than I do. I go to Tuscaloosa and watch practice. I talk with the players and coaches. Because he lives a few hours away on the Gulf Coast, Snake calls the coaches during the week and has lengthy meetings with them on the phone. As a result, when he comes to the booth, he has different types of notes than I do.

He'll say things like, "Here's what we're looking at in a third and such and such situation and what our options are going to be depending upon where the defensive backs from the other team are lined up. Are they man-to-man? Are they zone?" During the game he sketches and diagrams plays that he refers to during the broadcast.

Kenny's presence, without question, has made me a far better broadcaster. No matter how much I prepare, there are certain elements I can never bring to a broadcast. I've never taken a snap under center in the SEC or the NFL. The guy wears a Super Bowl ring. I'm smart enough to know what it is that I don't know (if you know what I mean). Kenny can explain it, explain it clearly, and do it in ten to twelve seconds before we have to set up the next play. He's that good. End of discussion.

We work really well together because, first of all, we have an excellent rapport. We laugh and joke. We don't get profane. (At least not on the air.) After all, this is a family show! In general, we have a blast. I like the way Kenny puts things. If we're talking about a certain NFL player, he'll say, "Yeah. I've been underneath him a few times." Or if the quarterback gets hit he'll say, "Now, that'll knock the taste out of your mouth!"

The other thing is, I think it helps that we look at the game totally differently. I'm a describer. He's a strategist. I describe what goes on, I follow, I see. He looks at the game like a quarterback does. And he has the ability of any well-trained, experienced analyst.

A good color man has to have a keen knowledge of the subject, particularly on radio. It's different on TV where you're adding captions to pictures and talking over the next play as the fans are watching it. But on radio, you've got twelve seconds to get in, analyze it, and get out. You're setting it up for the play-by-play guy so you've got to get out quick!

The color guy needs to explain what happened in such a way that keeps the veteran listener entertained but at the same time makes it digestible for the newcomer or casual fan. Again, you only have twelve seconds. It's not at all easy. And Snake nails it.

The biggest compliments we get as broadcasters are fans listening to our broadcasts—even when they're actually sitting in the stadium. I love to look down into the grandstands from our booth and see all the people with headsets on. They're at the ballgame—live and in person—but they're still listening to us! I can see them laughing or nodding and sometimes they'll turn around, look up toward our booth, and wave or give us a thumbs-up. What a hoot.

People at home also turn down the TV sound and turn on the radio when watching the game. I understand why they do this. The radio broadcast is a little more thorough. It's slanted towards Alabama and by now, Snake and I are like an old pair of broken-in loafers. People are used to us. They know we know the players and that makes them comfortable.

Why else is our broadcast as good as it is? (If I may say so myself!) It's because of our support crew. Tom Brokaw, late of *NBC Nightly News*, said it best when he signed off from his program for the last time in early December 2004. Brokaw said, "This is a huge team effort. I am the most conspicuous part of the team, but make no mistake about it, it's a huge team effort." So it is with the Crimson Tide Sports Network.

Seated behind Snake and myself during each broadcast is our engineer/producer, Tom Stipe. On Fridays before game days, home and away, Tom reports to the broadcast booth to begin the tedious job of setting up the equipment. Wires upon wires. Cables upon cables. The latest in sophisticated wireless gear, mixers, and studio hookups. It's quite a production. Later, Tom heads down to the locker room to check on transmission lines that will be used on our postgame show.

Tom sees to it that we don't have any technical flaws, which is good because in this age of digital audio transmission, every flaw is magnified. Let's face it, Snake and I work during a game, but Tom *really* works.

Aloha from Honolulu. (Left to right): Butch Owens, The Snake, Tom Roberts, Tom Stipe, and ol' Eli.

Standing behind Snake and me is our spotter, "Butch" Owens. His real name is Nelson (he said I wouldn't have the guts to put that in this book), and he is one of the most vital cogs in our operation. Butch has worked with me since the middle of the 1989 season. It doesn't matter which league or which network I'm working for, Alabama, NBC, CBS, TNN, or Sports USA Radio, if I'm doing a football game (college, NFL, arena) "Butchie Boy" is my spotter. What does a spotter do?

Butch helps "spot" certain things on every play. He keeps me current on substitutions. He pinpoints the tacklers. He'll watch for key blocks away from the ball that I might not have seen. He relays information to me via a series of hand and arm signals coupled with his pointing to a specially prepared spotting chart that I make for every team.

It's to the point now that I could miss a play totally and recreate it entirely through Butch's hand signals. Often, Butch will write me a note about which play ought to be called next, and, son of a gun, that's the play that'll be run. There is probably no one person more responsible for my growth as a football broadcaster than Butch Owens.

Statistician Brian Roberts sits to my left during every broadcast. Just like Butch, Brian works with me on all of my football broadcasts—Alabama, NFL, all of them. He is a walking, talking, Univac computer. He is accurate and quick, and he has an uncanny feel for what little statistical tidbit would fit into a broadcast at a given moment. Other than the obvious game-related stats, Brian keeps track of career numbers. Who is passing whom on an all-time list of one sort or another. The boy is good! He keeps some strange hours, but he's good.

And then there's Tom Roberts, our sideline reporter (among his many other duties). For years, Tom was the network's statistician before he moved to the sidelines and handed the stat job over to his son Brian. I have to stress, this was not nepotism. Indeed, Brian was deserving of the job. Before he was hired, Brian worked in the university sports information office keeping stats of televised ball games. He's great with numbers and has been an outstanding asset.

Like me, Tom Roberts is a lifelong broadcaster. From on-air TV newscasts to news director to broadcast management, Tom has been in this racket forever. On game day Tom anchors our pregame, halftime and postgame coverage, and he also fills the vital role of sideline reporter. He brings the emotion of being "right down there among them" to our listeners.

Photo courtesy of the Paul W. Bryant Museum, the University of Alabama.

Basketball color man and football pre-game host and sideline reporter, Tom Roberts.

Tom Roberts and Tom Stipe continually talk during the game. It was midseason in 2004 when all of a sudden, wide receiver Tyrone Prothro was lined up at quarterback. Instantly, Tom Roberts began yelling (off air, into Tom Stipe's headphone) "Prothro at quarterback! Prothro at quarterback!"

Immediately, Tom Stipe relays the information via our closed circuit communications loop, "Prothro at QB . . . That's Prothro!" Butch Owens, also seeing the swap at QB, begins gesturing wildly like a "pointer in heat" while at the same time I, too, notice that Pennington is out and Prothro is in. That's how our team works.

I know that I'm not the best football broadcaster in the world. I do alright, but I am comforted in knowing that my back is always covered by our crew. If Tom, Tom, Butch, or Brian tell me something, I use it on-air without a second thought. I trust them all implicitly. We're all great friends and blessed to be living a life that one could only dream about.

This crew and I feel a huge responsibility to the fans listening in the stadium as well as the fans who aren't in the stadium. There are people who can't come out to games because they're working or they're sick, or they can't afford tickets. I picture those folks in my mind's eye when I get to work on game day.

Radio has always played an enormous part in Alabama football. During the early championships and first days of Bear Bryant, the games weren't televised. In the late fifties, there was no such thing as ESPN. There were just the over-the-air networks that featured maybe one football game per week. This was for the whole country! In 1957 and 1958, not one Alabama game was televised.

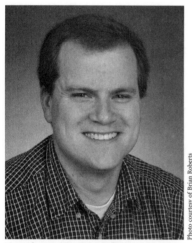

Photo courtesy of Brian Roberts

Network statistician Brian Roberts.

There was very limited TV coverage in those days, so when Alabama played away games, the radio network was your golden connection if you were not one of the lucky few who could travel and get a ticket to the opposing team's stadium. There was no such thing as satellite TV or videotape. Everything was shot on film. Film took time to develop. So the radio was it.

Longtime Alabama assistant coach Clem Gryska, who came to work for Coach Bryant in 1960, remembers having the radio on every weekend before he began attending every game in person.

"I would park the car in the carport," Gryska said, "turn the radio on and wash the car on Saturday afternoon. I'd turn the hose on, then stop it when I heard the volume of the crowd go up!"

These days, Alabama games are broadcast on stations affiliated with the Crimson Tide Sports Network, which carries the Alabama games (as well as the pregame and postgame shows, and *The Coach Mike Shula Show*) on some sixty stations. But this network, which is now a corporate conglomerate consisting of both radio and TV holdings, had some truly humble beginnings.

Bert Bank, at age ninety, is our distinguished producer emeritus and still sits in the booth with us on game days. He got the radio ball rolling in Tuscaloosa in 1953.

"Lionel Baxter, an outstanding broadcaster at WAPI in Birmingham, asked me to start the network," Bank said. "I had the only FM station in Tuscaloosa at the time. There weren't but two stations carrying Alabama football then, and he wanted the broadcast to originate in Tuscaloosa. Well, I was glad to do it. At the very least, I wanted to get the Alabama games for my station."

Photo courtesy of the Paul W. Bryant Museum, the University of Alabama.

Network founder Bert Bank.

The first year, Bert barely got his expenses covered. The next year, he was paid a salary. He hired announcers, began producing shows to go along with the football broadcast, and the network was under way.

Bert had the enormous challenge of starting the radio network during Alabama's less-than-victorious era. In 1953 Coach Red Drew's team went 6-3-3, followed by the 1954 season in which the team went 4-5-2. Then of course the next few years were Bama's worst ever—they won just four games in three years. True, fans of the Crimson Tide are loyal, but try selling radio ads or getting additional stations to sign on to the broadcast in this environment!

If anyone was up to a challenge, it was Bert Bank. As a young man and graduate of the University of Alabama, he planned to go to law school. When World War II broke out, however, he joined the Air Force instead. Bert has the incredible distinction of being a survivor of the Bataan Death March. He was held as a POW in Japanese camps for several years. He still speaks to veterans' groups and wrote a book about his experiences. After working in radio for years, he went on to serve in the Alabama legislature. Among his many accomplishments there was passing a bill renaming Denny Stadium as "Bryant-Denny Stadium" in 1975. What an inspirational man.

A few years into Bert's radio career, Alabama hired Paul W. "Bear" Bryant to be its new head coach. Bert knew right away this was terrific news for the school, the team, and the network.

"During our first meeting," Bert said, "Bryant asked me how many stations we had on the broadcast. I said five. He said, 'I don't care if a town only has fifty people. If they have a radio station, I want to be on it.'"

Bert told the coach in order to accomplish that, the team would have to win. Coach Bryant jumped out of his chair and said, "Crank it up, boy. I win!"

As Bert, and everyone else now knows, Bryant was true to his word.

"He knew one thing," Bert said, "and that was to beat you. I played golf with him, and if you beat him one day, you can bet your butt he'll be out there tomorrow looking for you, wanting to get his money back!"

Coach Bryant turned his team into winners immediately. Suddenly, it was no problem signing on new stations and sponsors. Well, almost no problem.

"One day, I asked him to come down and talk to a new sponsor," Bert remembered. "I said, Paul, I have a guy coming from Golden Flake potato chips. They're a big, big sponsor and I want you to be nice. If you've got any charm, please show it today!"

Happily, Golden Flake is still a major Alabama sponsor to this day. (And if I may say so, the makers of the best potato chips and pretzels anywhere.)

With a little help from the winning teams of the Bryant era and beyond, the Crimson Tide Sports Network now broadcasts Alabama games all over the state—and then some—every football Saturday. Few fans can travel to every out-of-town game, especially when they are played far away. So it's a thrill to serve as the fans' link to the team.

I feel honored to have the chance to do the job that the legendary John Forney did as the Voice of the Tide for thirty years. Our broadcasting booth is named after him because he was the one who was at the helm during radio's glory days.

John Forney was the conduit. He was the man who brought Bear Bryant into people's living rooms through the sixties and seventies, at a time when we still got very little TV coverage and before there was such a thing as ESPN or the Deuce (ESPN2).

A young John Forney.

Photo courtesy of the Paul W. Bryant Museum, the University of Alabama.

The thing is, radio still matters. After all this time, people still tune in. What an absolutely spectacular medium—radio is theater of the mind, really. I have the responsibility and, hopefully, the ability to describe the color of the pewter grey sky overhead, the color of the uniforms, the smells and the sounds. I always work with the windows of our booth wide open so I can be a part of things, so I can "feel" the game. Hopefully, people benefit from that.

I was reminded of the importance of radio a while ago when coach Mike Shula shared a wonderful letter he got from a soldier serving in Iraq. On the air we always say, "Hello to Armed Forces Radio." But this time we got some feedback that these guys in the middle of some Godforsaken part of the desert had found a way to log onto the computer and pick up our broadcast.

It really touched me. The guy wrote, "When Eli Gold's voice starts intoning from the stadium, we're transformed to the ballpark. I'm an Alabama fan and I'm sitting next to an Auburn fan doing the same job. We're arguing with a Tennessee fan and guys from the PAC-10, and it's a little touch of home."

What a scene. Here are guys brushing aside sand fleas and trying to tune out mortar rounds while putting one ear up to the speaker to pick up our broadcast. It kind of puts it in perspective. And makes me want to keep doing this for a hundred more years.

GREAT VOICES OF THE CRIMSON TIDE

DICK REID   **MAURY FARRELL**   **DAVE OVERTON**

FRANK BRUCE   **LELAND CHILDS**   **MEL ALLEN**

CHARLEY ZEANAH   **GABBY BELL**   **DOUG LAYTON**

STAN SIEGAL   **PAUL KENNEDY**   **JERRY DUNCAN**

KENNY STABLER   **ELI GOLD**

Photos courtesy of the Paul W. Bryant Museum, the University of Alabama.

T W O

Who's That
Denny Guy?

Chiming In

I ADMIT IT. I TEND TO LOOK AT THE WORLD THROUGH CRIMSON-colored glasses. But how can you not? On a sunny fall day on the campus of the University of Alabama, the view is just spectacular.

Bryant-Denny Stadium, the focal point of the campus, is always an impressive sight, especially when packed full of crimson-wearing fans. The bright green field is lush and ready. The flags are flapping in the wind. Then, when the cluster of Bama players come bursting from their tunnel, well, it's quite a sight.

For my money, the finest stadium in the land: Bryant-Denny in Tuscaloosa.

Photo courtesy of Kent Gidley, the University of Alabama.

On game days the acreage surrounding the stadium is always a bastion of activity. The undisputed hub of all this activity is the quad, a large open area, where thousands of Bama fans set up tents, tables, and booths in order to properly prepare for the game. (The RVers set up several days before, but that's another story.)

On the quad, they get up early and get busy putting up crimson and white bunting and big, blow-up Big Al's. They proudly display their custom-made signs ("B.U.T.T.: Bama's Ultimate Tailgate Team," "Ted and Judy say, 'Roll Tide!'"). They set up smokers, fill their coolers, and hook up their satellite dishes and radios to catch the pregame action. They blast "Sweet Home Alabama" and "Yea Alabama" from their CD players and cheer "Roll Tide!" and wave to passersby.

I never get over it. It's truly incredible.

Denny Chimes.

Photo courtesy of Kent Gidley, the University of Alabama.

In the middle of this beehive, is an impressive structure called Denny Chimes. You can't miss it. It's just across from the president's mansion. This university landmark is a 115-foot-tall clock tower from which chimes intermittently ring out. At the base of Denny Chimes, surrounding it on all sides, is the Walk of Champions, a cement walkway created to honor the team captains of the Alabama football teams, past and present. Every spring the current captains place a hand and cleat-wearing foot in the wet cement next to their names. There's over a hundred years' worth of Alabama football history represented by these names: Gilmer, Richeson, Croom, Baumhower. Offense. Defense. They're all there. The list goes on and on.

Fans love to walk by and place their hands into the prints of past gridiron stars. They love to gather at the base of Denny Chimes to get a better view of their Crimson and White world.

When a student stands waiting for a friend after telling her to "Meet me at Denny Chimes," or an alumnus strolls along the Walk of Champions, do they ever think about the man named Denny? Do any of us know who he was? He was obviously important enough to have his name emblazoned on the above-mentioned chimes, not to mention the football stadium. Up until 1975, when Coach Bryant's name was added, the grand structure everyone now knows as Bryant-Denny Stadium was just plain Denny Stadium.

So who was this Denny guy?

Dr. George Hutcheson Denny became president of the University of Alabama in 1912. He came from Virginia, having earned his undergraduate degree at Hampden-Sydney College and his PhD at the University of Virginia, where, incidentally, football was growing in popularity.

While going to school "back east," Dr. Denny grew to love football and noticed that a school could get a great deal of national press coverage if they fielded a good team. He saw football as a means to help Alabama grow in reputation and stature. Employing a combination of charm and good organizational skills, Dr. Denny went to work.

Dr. George Hutcheson Denny, University President (1912-1936).

Photo courtesy of the William Stanley Hoole Special Collections Library, the University of Alabama.

His first order of business was to secure better facilities for the fledgling team. In 1912 the Crimson Tide held their practices in front of the library on the grassy area that is now the quad. Denny thought it more suitable for them to have an actual field. (A year or two later they got it and named it "Denny Field.")

The football of 1912 was a very different game than the one played today. Players pictured in the quaint, sepia-toned photos of the early twentieth-century Alabama teams look practically like choirboys. I mean, come on! These guys didn't even wear helmets! They wore turtleneck sweaters with the big red letters "UA" sewn on the front. They stuffed a little cotton around their shoulders for "padding." How tough a game could it have been?

If newspaper accounts and history books are to be believed, the college football games of this era were often brutal, sloppy, and violent affairs. There are many accounts of serious injuries and even deaths. The fans, and even the coaches and refs (sometimes they were one and the same!) often acted in a less-than-dignified manner.

The mayhem began in 1869. The first official college football game is said to have taken place on November 6 of that year, matching Princeton and Rutgers in New Brunswick, New Jersey. The game played that day resembled rugby more than football—the rules of possession, downs, and even the concept of using one's hands had yet to fully evolve.

It is said that a Rutgers professor, who was passing by on his bicycle stopped to watch the game for a moment. Evidently, he didn't like what he saw. "You men will come to no Christian end!" he shouted, before pedaling away.

Maybe the professor caught sight of the prevailing playing technique of the day, "the flying wedge." This was a formation where players held hands or locked arms and charged at the opposition full speed, keeping the ball carrier "safe" in the so-called pocket. *Safe* was a relative word, though.

Imagine players linked at the elbow to their teammates, crashing full speed into other players also moving full steam. With no pads. This practice, which lasted into the early 1900s, proved to be so controversial that even President Teddy Roosevelt got involved and managed to convince schools to ban it.

Football was first introduced to Bama students by William G. Little, a Livingston, Alabama, native who transferred to the university from

Phillips-Exeter Academy in Andover, Massachusetts, where people loved the sport played with the strange pigskin ball.

Little managed to put together a team of about a dozen players. They recruited Eugene Beaumont, who learned the game in Pennsylvania, to be their coach. Little, who is said to have been the biggest man on the team (depending on which account you believe—he is listed at anywhere from 173 to 220 pounds), was named captain. Regardless of his actual poundage, there is evidence that Little enjoyed his grub. Winston Groom, author of *The Crimson Tide: An Illustrated History of Football at the University of Alabama*, dug up this quote from Little: "Players will be forced to live a most ascetic life, on a diet of rare beef and pork, to say nothing of rice pudding for dessert, for additional courage and fortitude, to stand the bumps and injuries."

Either Little thought a man needed extra natural padding in those days of few, if any, pads, or he believed food would motivate his team. (I'm reminded of a story John Hannah liked to tell about steak in the chow line being the best motivator he'd ever known. But that was still decades away.)

Little also said, "Football is the game of the future in college life." This, of course, turned out to be prophetic. Baseball was already popular on the Alabama campus in the late 1800s. But when Dr. Denny arrived, football would move to the forefront.

Little and his team played the first official game of Alabama football on November 11, 1892. If we think some of those directional "Southeastern North State" schools are perceived as cupcakes, check out

Photo courtesy of the William Stanley Hoole Special Collections Library, the University of Alabama.

University President Denny giving a fiery speech with a young fan looking on.

Bama's first opponent: Birmingham High School. Nonetheless, when the Cadets of Alabama (as Bama was known back then) carried the day with a 56-0 victory, a tradition was born.

Many people looked down on this uncouth, unfamiliar, rowdy northern sport when it was first introduced to Alabama. But if people had known what fine, upstanding young men would emerge from this first team, maybe they would have thought differently. That first squad of just over a dozen players included a fullback, W. B. Bankhead, who would go on to become Speaker of the U.S. House of Representatives. Another player, Bibb Graves, would eventually serve two terms as Alabama governor. Their teammates' future vocations ranged from state senator, judge, and lawyer to physician and other assorted businessmen. Either they put something in the rice pudding or football was perhaps a bridge to future success.

As more opponents became available at other schools, Alabama football continued to evolve over the next few years. In 1893 the coach of the Crimson White (as they were being called at the time), Eli Abbott, also played fullback for the team. Unfortunately his efforts weren't enough to beat Auburn in the first-ever Iron Bowl matchup, played at Lakeview Park in Birmingham. Auburn won it, 32-22. (Note: during those years the team got a new coach almost every year. If the team beat Auburn, however, the coach usually got to keep his job.)

Interestingly, the late 1890s saw the introduction of cheerleaders—a very early version of them anyway. Women students, who had started attending the university during this time, were enlisted as "sponsors," even though a hilariously politically incorrect newspaper story of the day provided this caveat:

> There will be a large crowd of ladies, society belles, and school girls to wear the colors of their favorites and to applaud the good work of their eleven. Of course they won't understand anything about the game, but that doesn't make any difference, for they will cheer and enjoy it as much as if they were critical onlookers.

A few years later, in 1897, the team actually skipped the season due to the Spanish-American War. But they soon returned to the field and, in 1902 a sportswriter borrowed a phrase from a Rudyard Kipling poem and dubbed them "the Thin Red Line."

John W. H. "Doc" Pollard coached the team in 1907. He was a tough man known for his brutal practices. Pollard, who stayed for four years, was in charge during the infamous 1907 Auburn game. The two rivals played a messy, muddy game in front of five thousand spectators, up to that point the largest crowd in Alabama football history. The game, which ended in a tie, has the dubious distinction of being the last one the two teams would play for forty years. Evidently, there were so many squabbles about money, refs, how many players could travel with the team, etc., that both sides got fed up and decided to scrap it. (Note: this was also the game that inspired a long-lasting nickname, when *Birmingham Age-Herald* sportswriter Hugh Roberts wrote, "The Alabama players rolled over their opponents like a Crimson Tide.")

Even though they wouldn't play Auburn for decades, Alabama found other opponents and new rivals. During this era arguably their biggest rival was Sewanee. They played Tennessee every year, too. In 1909, Bama beat the Vols, 10-0, much to the dismay of the Tennessee faithful, some of whom chased a ref out of the stadium and threw rocks at him until he rode away on a streetcar.

The 1912 Tennessee game was a memorable one indeed. Technically, this is counted as Alabama's first night game since it became so dark in the fourth quarter that the teams had to finish the game under the glare of car headlights. Obviously, Dr. Denny still had a ways to go to bring football into the modern era.

Denny's focus on the football program began to pay off quickly, though. The 1913 team went 6-3. More impressive perhaps was the fact that Bama outscored its opponents 188-40. That same year tackle W. T. "Bully" Vandegraaff, one of Bama's first big stars, became the University's first All-American. Vandegraaff is an absolute legend in Alabama football. As the famous story goes, Vandegraaff nearly lost an ear playing against (who else?) Tennessee. Tennessee lineman Bull Bayer told a reporter, "His ear had a real nasty cut, and it was dangling from his head, bleeding badly. He grabbed his own ear and tried to yank it from his head. His teammates stopped him and the managers bandaged him. Man, was that guy a tough one. He wanted to tear off his own ear so he could keep playing." (Alright, stop squirming and making faces and read on!)

By this time, many players were wearing "helmets," which were really just thin, leather headpieces designed to protect the ears. Evidently Vandegraaff was not one of them!

The year President Denny arrived on campus, Bama's coach was Dorset Vandeventer "D. V." Graves, who stayed for four years. He accumulated a winning record (21-12-3) during his four years at Alabama, and is often remembered for his comments about his small-in-stature, big-on-heart team of 1912:

> In September, the squad looked light and of poor physical development. Everything was discouraging. I had not yet become familiar with the Alabama Spirit—that indescribable something which made the efforts of a light team bring seemingly impossible results.

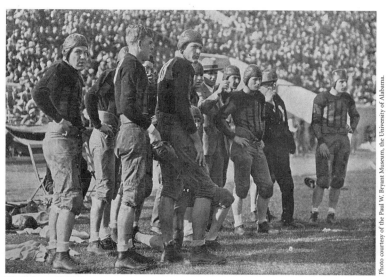

The Crimson Tide of yore.

COACH GRAVES LEFT IN 1914 AFTER FOUR YEARS, IN THOSE DAYS A long tenure for a coach, most of whom served one year and then moved on. Denny hoped to change that. He was the first president to look at the big picture—to really look ahead past the season at hand. He definitely thought strong and consistent leadership was important for the program. That's why Denny got heavily involved in the head coach selection process.

Denny handpicked Graves's successor, the burly 250-pound, cigar-chomping Thomas Kelley, to head up the team in 1915. Kelley had gone to school at the University of Chicago, a tremendous football school whose coach was none other than Amos Alonzo Stagg, the man whose "winningest" record Bear Bryant would overtake many years later.

Kelley's first team won its first four games, only to see Kelley stricken with typhoid fever, forcing him to sit out the rest of the year. The athletics director and team captain took over the coaching role for the rest of the season, which ended successfully. Bama went 6-2, shutting out every team they beat except Sewanee.

Coach Kelley returned in 1916, but the illness had taken its toll. (He lost an astonishing one hundred pounds.) He coached two more winning seasons, and then the Tide took a year off in 1918 due to World War I.

For the 1919 season Dr. Denny again hand-selected the new head coach— Xen Scott. The choice was controversial at first, mainly because Scott had never coached before. He was a horseracing writer from Cleveland! Apparently, President Denny thought a writer could coach!

Because Scott was an incredibly easygoing man, many people doubted he would be able to instill the discipline necessary to win. But he was a great strategist, and critics were silenced when Scott's 1919 team posted the best record to date for a Bama team (8-1). The 1920 season was even better (10-1). Scott went on to coach two more winning seasons.

Photo courtesy of the Paul W. Bryant Museum, the University of Alabama.

Coach Wallace Wade.

In 1923 Scott left for reasons that remain somewhat unclear—he likely was in ill health at the time, considering that he passed away from cancer not long after he left Alabama. It was then that Denny brought in a coach who would absolutely insure Alabama's football legacy: Wallace Wade.

With Denny's support, Wade oversaw Alabama's first glory period, an incredible eight-season run that produced national titles in 1925, 1926, and 1930. Wade made college football history when his 1925 squad became the first southern team to play in the Rose Bowl. And they won!

When Wade left in 1931, Denny turned to Frank Thomas, who would rack up even more titles, records, and accolades than Coach Wade.

President Denny retired in 1936 after serving as president for twenty-five years, the longest term of any University of Alabama president. When Denny came to Alabama, five hundred students were enrolled at the school. The year he retired, there were nearly five thousand. Many people credit the university's growth in part to Denny's support of the football program, which had been virtually nonexistent in 1912 and would, during his tenure, explode to produce five national championships.

Alabama's official party at the 1926 Rose Bowl included Dr. George Denny (holding roses) and Southern Conference President, Dr. S.V. Sanford.

Denny once told a reporter about a secret ambition: "I would like to coach a football team or manage a baseball club when I finish as university president," he said. "Athletics have always appealed to me, and I would just like to manage one baseball club."

Sadly, Denny retired under a cloud of controversy involving some members of the faculty and the state legislature who resented his extreme emphasis on athletics. According to the press reports of the day, he also had weathered his share of struggles within the athletic department. Winners like Wallace Wade and Frank Thomas had strong personalities and sometimes did not appreciate what could have been perceived as too much input from the university president.

Nonetheless, the day Denny Stadium was dedicated in 1929, Dr. Denny's legacy was secured. How fitting that the monument that bears his name is surrounded by the hand and footprints of over a hundred years of Alabama football stars.

George Hutcheson Denny passed away in 1955 at age eighty-four, two years before Bear Bryant would arrive as head coach at Alabama. No doubt he would have beamed with pride over what was to come.

Wade's successor, Coach Frank Thomas.

THREE

The Wallace Wade Era

Winning Wade

IF ONE HAD TO PINPOINT WHEN THE TRUE GLORY ERA OF ALABAMA football began, it would be the moment when thirty-one-year-old Wallace Wade, the youngest Bama coach to date, arrived in Tuscaloosa in 1923 to take over as head coach.

Wallace Wade made college football history.

Photo courtesy of the Paul W. Bryant Museum, the University of Alabama.

Coach Wade not only compiled an impressive record (61-13-3) during his seven-year reign, he also proceeded to make college football history by taking his 1925 undefeated team to the Rose Bowl. (This was the first southern team to ever play on New Year's Day in Pasadena. Bama won the game and brought home the national title—another first.)

Wade's teams played in three Rose Bowls and won three national titles. Incredible accomplishments for a seven-year period. No question, Wade was a winner. But the moment that ultimately defined him as a coach may have come when his team lost.

Wallace Wade's teams didn't lose very often. In 1925 and 1926 the Crimson Tide completed back-to-back undefeated seasons. Both these teams won the Southern Conference championship and national title. Then, in 1927, after going into the season with an incredible twenty-two consecutive victories, the team went 5-4-1.

One can imagine the grumblings of the now-spoiled Alabama fans, even though Wade tried to put a positive spin on the season. In a 1927 newspaper story, a reporter wrote that, "Coach Wade is mighty proud of his team this year despite the fact that it has lost and he sees the silver lining even to that cloud, because he says that the student body of the University of Alabama has begun to sit up and take notice now that they've seen the team CAN lose—for they'd got so used to winning that they took things sort of as a matter of course." (Author's note: They must not have been big on punctuation, or breathing for that matter, back in those days.)

Since Wade came to town, they now expected to win. But one can also imagine the fans excusing this one "down" year. After all, most of the star players had graduated at the end of 1926. Few members of the 1927 squad had any varsity experience. Everybody deserves time to rebuild.

The team showed slight improvement in 1928, finishing 6-3. There was more grumbling from fans, though. Especially after a loss to Tennessee. This just wouldn't do! *This is Alabama after all!* Then, in 1929, when the team again finished with an "OK for other schools but not up to snuff for Alabama" record of 6-3, the grumblings grew to a loud roar.

By having such unparalleled success early on, Wade had created his own impossible act to follow. He heard the criticism and was apparently deeply affected by it. At the end of the 1929 season, the *Birmingham News* broke the incredible story that Wallace Wade had accepted the head coaching job at Duke University. What was truly incredible, though, was the fact that he would not start his new position until 1931. He had a contract and would complete the 1930 season at Alabama first. This is unfathomable in today's world of broken contracts and bolting to the highest bidder.

Disappointed by his own performance, (he often said, "The best you can do is not good enough unless it does the job") and by his negative word of mouth, Wade decided it was time to move on. Then, in his final showing

Wade proved himself to be the true winner that he was when he proceeded to lead his team to perhaps the best season he tallied under his watch.

It's almost as if he was unburdened by the fact that he knew he was leaving. (Was he thinking they won't have Wallace Wade to kick around anymore?) It also seems as though this great, winning coach was determined to make one last stand. And in 1930, his final season at Alabama, he did just that.

Bama gets two yards versus Stanford in the 1927 Rose Bowl.

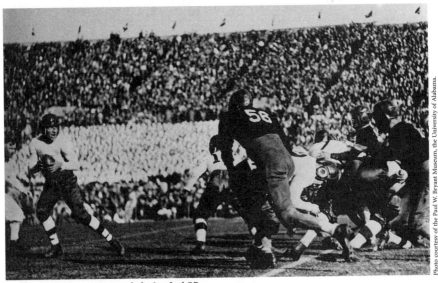

Wu Winslett (#56) comes in to rush the Stanford QB.

The 1930 squad won the Southern Conference title, and, after crushing Washington State, 24-0, in the Rose Bowl, they also brought home the national title. Alabama's opponents scored only thirteen points on them all year long, while the Tide put 247 points on the board. The numbers were just staggering.

But Alabama did more than just pile up points during the 1930 season. This was the year the school got the mascot that we have to this day. After the team's magnificent victory over Ole Miss, *Atlanta Journal* sportswriter Everett Strupper wrote: "That Alabama team of 1930 is a typical (Coach) Wade machine, powerful, big, tough, fast, aggressive, well-schooled in fundamentals and the best-blocking team for this early in the season that I have ever seen. When those big brutes hit you I mean you go down and stay down, often for an additional two minutes."

Strupper went on: "Coach Wade started his second team that was plenty big and they went right to their knitting scoring a touchdown in the first quarter against one of the best fighting small lines that I have ever seen. For Ole Miss was truly battling the big boys for every inch of the ground. At the end of the quarter, the earth started to tremble, there was a distant rumble that continued to grow. Some excited fan in the stands bellowed, 'Hold your horses, the ELEPHANTS are coming,' and out stomped the Alabama varsity."

Strupper continued to use the name, "Red Elephants" all season long. When other journalists followed suit, that's how Bama got the Red Elephants who came to be symbolized by Big Al. Of course, Alabama still goes by the proud nickname of "the Crimson Tide." But a school needs a mascot. And how in the world are you going to

Photo courtesy of the Paul W. Bryant Museum, the University of Alabama.

Bama beat Washington State 24-0 in the 1931 Rose Bowl.

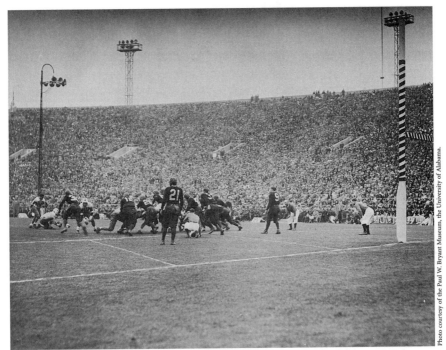

Photo courtesy of the Paul W. Bryant Museum, the University of Alabama.

Much like today, Bama always plays in front of sell-out crowds. This one was on January 1, 1931 in Pasadena.

dress a guy up like a "tide"? So Big Al and the Crimson Tide work together. The more the merrier.

"Working Together" was a great theme for Wade's 1930 team. During his final game, the 1931 Rose Bowl, Coach Wade showed just how well his team could execute a plan. He surprised the Tide's Rose Bowl rival, Washington State, by starting the game with all backup players. By the time the starters took over in the second quarter, rested and raring to go, Bama had already scored three touchdowns.

Evidently, Wade employed this unorthodox technique often during the 1930 season. In later years he explained his reasoning to reporter Clyde Bolton: "We were so deep that we started the second team in every game, including the Rose Bowl. They always played the first quarter. There were several reasons we did that. One was psychological. You see, that second team was able to hold everybody scoreless the whole year. We knew it would help us for an opponent to play the second team and not score and then know we were sending in the first string."

During the Rose Bowl, Wade expanded on his philosophy of starting the second-stringers and continued to shift players and confound Washington throughout the game. (Interesting note: the final field goal of the game was kicked by J. B. "Ears" Whitworth, who would go on to become Bama's head coach in the fifties.)

The 1931 Rose Bowl was quite a swan song for Wade. After seven seasons in which he brought home three national championships, took his team to three Rose Bowls and virtually put all of Southern Football on the map, Wade left town with his head up high.

WILLIAM WALLACE WADE WAS RAISED IN RURAL TENNESSEE, ONE OF five sons of a prosperous farmer. He later headed up north to Chicago for prep school, then went east to attend Brown University. He was a right guard—and a star—on Brown's football team, which just happened to play in the second-ever Rose Bowl, in 1916. His team lost.

When Wade became head coach at Alabama and took his team to the Rose Bowl in 1927, he became the first man ever to both play and coach in a Rose Bowl game.

After graduation, Wade joined the army and went on to serve as a captain in the cavalry. He was discharged in 1919 and took a job coaching the football team at Fitzgerald-Clarke, a prep school in Tullahoma, Tennessee. His team did well. In two seasons they won fifteen and lost two. Wade's performance caught the attention of Vanderbilt's Dan McGugin, who hired him immediately.

During the two seasons Wade was at Vanderbilt, the Commodores went undefeated. Then, in 1923 McGugin recommended Wade to the University of Alabama's football-friendly president, George Denny, who after learning of then coach Xen Scott's severe illness, was actively searching for a new head coach.

It wasn't long before Wade was hired and had moved to Tuscaloosa.

Wade's predecessor, Scott, had a winning record despite his reputation for short, relatively undemanding practices and a very nice, approachable personality. It is well documented that he was a laid-back guy who had mostly positive things to say to his players and counted on his assistants to dole out any discipline.

Then came Wade. Alabama's new head coach did not believe in too much praise. He was quoted as saying, "Nobody ever got back-slapped into anything."

Wade believed in simple hard work (goodbye to short practices) and efficiency. He reportedly thought about football—and only football—day and night. He asked for complete dedication and production from his players and coaches. He didn't tolerate any excuses. He was a tough guy.

Although it has all the makings of a myth, there is another quote often attributed to Wade. Evidently, Coach Wade approached an injured player and asked him what was the matter.

Johnny Mack Brown (left) and Pooley Hubert (right) helped build the Tide into a dynasty.

The player said, "I think my leg is broken." The coach responded, "Well, you've got another one, haven't you?"

Bill Baty, who played three seasons for Xen Scott and then his senior year under Wade in 1923, once told a reporter about Wade's brand of tough love.

"Wade was a disciplinarian of the first order," Baty said. "He coached a lot through fear rather than through warmth or persuasion." But like many of his fellow players, Baty ultimately concluded that Wade's ways were effective, even appreciated.

From touchdowns to Hollywood fame: Johnny Mack Brown.

"I remember one time Wade called me into his office and read me up and down the back," Baty said. "He said, 'I think you're loafing, and if you are you won't last long on this team. You either get going or you're finished. I think what's eating on you is that you thought you'd get elected captain and you weren't.' Wade was real smart. He hit it right on the nail. He said get going or turn in your suit and I said I'd get going."

Many successful head coaches are no-nonsense guys. Wade, like the great Bama coaches who came after him, Frank Thomas, Bear Bryant, and Gene Stallings, was a straight shooter who put football first. Evidently, he thought about football all the time and really didn't enjoy talking about much else.

In a 1927 column, *Birmingham News-Age Herald* reporter Dolly Dalyrymple wrote about Coach Wade and his one-track mind: "Like the 'Lone Eagle' who likes to talk only about aviation, we were told Coach Wade cares to talk only about football."

In the flowery prose of her day, Ms. Dalyrymple continued: "Coach Wade is one of the most modest of men; he is very reticent about himself—just as we'd been told—but he is ever ready to talk about football and about the Crimson Tide, which is the pride of his life."

In the article, Coach Wade explained his philosophy: "What I try to do is get the very best out of every boy who becomes a member of the Crimson Tide team. I try to impress upon boys that I am fair and square with them; I never try to appeal to their sentiment. I never ask a boy to try to win a game for my sake, but on the other hand put him on his mettle to do his

Photo courtesy of the Paul W. Bryant Museum, the University of Alabama.

En route to one of Coach Wallace Wades 61 career wins at Bama.

level best and failing, he feels the discomfort of not having done his duty, measuring up to the best that is in him.

"A coach gets or fails to get results on account of his ability to handle boys; he must inspire them with confidence and enthusiasm, which is far more important than his technical training."

According to press reports at the time, people were speculating as to exactly how Coach Wade was inspiring his players. One rumor said that Wade's pregame reading requirement for his team was no less than Dante's *Inferno*, complete with images of the fires of Hell. Wade himself dispelled this tall tale: "Football players, when they have done their work satisfactorily as far as the curriculum goes and have done their best work on the team, have very little time for reading, save that which goes in the regular educational course," Wade said. Then adding perhaps a glimmer of humor he said, "Of course, I always advocate the highest class of literature for college boys."

With or without Dante, Wade apparently inspired his team quite successfully. During his first season as head coach, he took his team, which at the beginning of the season boasted only two players with more than a year's experience, to a 7-2-1 finish. The Tide racked up 222 points and held their opponents to just fifty. They beat Sewanee, their archrival during the twenties, in a 7-0 battle that turned around when star halfback Johnny Mack Brown made a dazzling interception in the fourth quarter.

Star halfback Johnny Mack.

Photo courtesy of the Paul W. Bryant Museum, the University of Alabama.

Two Bama players, Al Clemens and Grant Gillis, were named All-Southern Conference that year. As the calendar flipped to 1924, there was every reason to be upbeat about the season to come. Wade felt that he and his players had come to a mutual understanding. Indeed, coach and team had meshed.

The Crimson Tide opened the 1924 season with a series of shutout wins against Union, Furman, Mississippi College, and Sewanee. The Tide then thrilled their fans with a 14-0 stomping of Georgia Tech in Atlanta.

Going into the game, Tech was heavily favored in the papers due to a recent win over Penn State and the fact that they had not lost to another southern team in over three years. Johnny Mack Brown made history during this game, gaining some 135 yards on just ten plays!

The Tide beat Ole Miss by an unheard-of final score of 61-0 and then beat Kentucky during homecoming, when Johnny Mack Brown was rewarded with a five-minute standing ovation after a spectacular ninety-nine-yard touchdown run.

Centre College beat Bama, 17-0, marring an otherwise perfect season in which the Crimson Tide finished 8-1 and won the Southern Conference championship. Three players—Johnny Mack Brown, Bill Buckler, and Pooley Hubert—were named All-Southern Conference.

All-American Allison T.S. "Pooley" Hubert.

Photo courtesy of the Paul W. Bryant Museum, the University of Alabama.

"Football is a lot like war," Coach Wade said after this incredible season. So the general and his gridiron troops returned to basic training to prepare for the following year.

The season of 1925 became the season that would set the bar for all future Bama teams (and other college teams) that would come after them. The Tide finished with a perfect 9-0 record and went on to become the first southern team ever to play in the Rose Bowl when they traveled to Pasadena to meet Washington on New Year's Day. This would have been fact enough to enter into the history books. But then Bama went and won it!

To say Alabama was the underdog in this match is like saying Rhode Island would be the underdog in a war against China. The snobbery and anti-southern bias were less than subtle.

One L.A. columnist deemed to call the Alabama players "Swamp Students," and even beloved humorist Will Rogers (who came around after the fact) weighed in ahead of time by calling the Tide a bunch of "Tusca-losers."

It was sweet revenge for Alabama and all southern teams (and possibly, all southerners) when Bama pulled off the thrilling 20-19 victory.

Coach Wade called this win the greatest thrill of his career.

The Rose Bowl win was big, big news. The front page of the *L.A. Examiner* from January 2, 1926, had a huge banner across the top: "Alabama beats Huskies, 20-19." The story, although filled with accurate facts of the exciting game, managed to get in just one more dig on the victorious Tide in its opening paragraph: "You wouldn't have given a nickel for Alabama's chances in the game with Washington as the second half opened this afternoon."

Pooley Hubert (#10) scores for Bama.

But it was how the story ended that really counts. And even better, this happy ending was really just the beginning. Incredibly, the Crimson Tide repeated its perfect season in 1926 and again traveled west to play in the Rose Bowl. This time, the team played Stanford to a 7-7 tie in a game that marked the first transcontinental radio broadcast (courtesy of NBC) of a sporting event.

Wade resigned as Alabama's head coach after the 1930 season. He went on to coach at Duke University for sixteen years. Incredibly, his coaching duties were interrupted in 1942 when he returned to military service for four years during World War II.

No one can argue that Coach Wallace Wade made his mark on the University of Alabama football program. He set a standard of excellence that still stands. He was old-fashioned and tough—his players were punished for even looking at girls—and the idea of having fun, even while in California for the Rose Bowl was unthinkable. It may be easy for me to say—I never played for Wade. But looking back, I guess we can all be glad that Coach Wade thought about football and nothing but football.

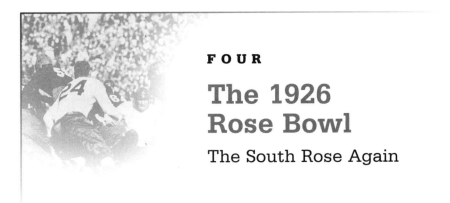

The 1926 Rose Bowl

The South Rose Again

AS HARD AS IT MAY BE TO BELIEVE, THERE WAS A TIME LONG, LONG ago when the words *southern* and *football* didn't really go together. In the early twentieth century, the words were never printed on the same page. But in 1925 Coach Wallace Wade led his University of Alabama football team to a perfect 9-0 record during the regular season. Then, he iced the proverbial gridiron cake by taking his team to Pasadena, California, to play in the Rose Bowl. No southern team had ever played in the prestigious Tournament of Roses New Year's Day game before.

This team not only played in the Rose Bowl, they won it and brought home Alabama's first national championship. And no doubt about it, this team made history. Not just for Alabama. They absolutely put all of southern football on the map. After 1926 the words *southern* and *football* would be frequent partners in print and in discussions between fans of college football for years to come.

Wallace Wade had taken over as Alabama head coach in 1923. During his first season, the team notched a respectable record of 7-2-1. The team steadily improved in 1924: they went 8-1 and won the Southern Conference championship.

All of Coach Wade's best-laid plans came together in 1925. This was his third season as head coach and he had quite a few returning starters, including star quarterback Pooley Hubert, supremely talented running back Johnny Mack Brown, and the magnificent end "Wu" Winslett.

Early in the season a reporter wrote: "Alabama has a great collection of backs. Coach Wade can shut his eyes and pick a great combination of backs from this group that cannot be equaled."

Understandably, Wade kept his eyes wide open all season long. There were just too many wonderful sights to see. Alabama totally annihilated their first three opponents. They beat Birmingham Southern (50-7), Union (53-0), and LSU (42-0). Next on their hit list was then archrival Sewanee. The Tide won their annual matchup, 27-0.

Perhaps Bama's biggest test that year came against undefeated Georgia Tech on October 24. The game was scoreless until Johnny Mack Brown caught and returned a punt fifty-five yards for a spectacular touchdown. His blockers were amazing; they knocked down virtually every Tech player, as well as the ref, to make room for their guy. Alabama won that game, 7-0. Incredibly, the next four Alabama victories, which finished the regular season, were all shutouts. In fact, Alabama's defense allowed only seven points all year. Incredible.

For the second year in a row, Bama beat out twenty-one other teams to win the Southern Conference championship. Quarterback Pooley Hubert was named conference MVP and was widely touted as the best quarterback to ever play in the South. At a team banquet, the 1925 squad was voted "the Greatest in Crimson Tide History."

Picture Day for Alabama prior to the 1926 Rose Bowl.

Photo courtesy of the Paul W. Bryant Museum, the University of Alabama.

The accolades were just being heaped on this magnificent ball club. But there was one more honor coming their way. After the regular season, Alabama was issued an invitation to represent the Southern Conference in the 1926 Rose Bowl.

It should be said that this invitation was issued quite reluctantly. In his book *The Crimson Tide*, Winston Groom reports that Alabama was not the Rose Bowl committee's first choice. In fact, they first invited Dartmouth, Yale, and then Colgate to play in their national championship game, but all three schools declined due to an edict from the American Association of University Professors that said, "Football promoted drinking, dishonesty, and poor academics." Apparently, there was pressure from the professors to do away with football altogether.

Despite one committee member's comment, "I've never heard of Alabama as a football team and can't take a chance on mixing a lemon with a rose," Alabama was in.

Coach Wade spent no time dwelling on the roundabout nature of the invitation. He was absolutely thrilled and immediately called a team meeting to bring the bowl bid before the players for their vote.

"Fellows, this is what a trip to the Rose Bowl means," Wade said. "There will be three weeks of tough, hard practice. I want you all to realize that to the full and think about it. But here's something else to remember. Southern collegiate football is not recognized as being anywhere near what it is in the East, West, and Midwest. So here's your chance to be part of history."

It was unanimous. Bama was Rose Bowl bound.

THE ROSE BOWL WAS A LATE ADDITION TO THE HISTORIC Tournament of Roses festivities, which were first celebrated in 1890. Pasadena's Valley Hunt Club, a group of folks who had moved from cities in the East and Midwest to sunny California, were anxious to show off the beautiful, mild winter weather in their adopted home.

"In New York, people are buried in snow," club member Charles F. Holder said at an early meeting of the group. "Here, our flowers are blooming, and our oranges are about to bear. Let's hold a festival to tell the world about our paradise."

With that, the Valley Hunt Club organized a New Year's Day parade featuring horse-drawn carriages covered with real flowers. Hence the name: Tournament of Roses. Other activities such as polo matches and tug-of-war contests went on throughout the day.

The Tournament of Roses Association was formed in 1895 to handle the growing festival, which had expanded over the years to include those celebrated California activities, such as ostrich and camel races. The parade began by featuring marching bands and, eventually, motorized floats. Today the floats are so intricate and complex that they often are built by professional float-builders and take up to a year to construct!

It was in 1902 that the committee decided to schedule a football game as the grand finale to the day. "Local" favorite Stanford University (not that Palo Alto is anywhere near Pasadena) was paired against the University of Michigan, which proceeded to crush the California team, 49-0. The blowout was such a bust that Roman-style chariot races were brought in to replace the ball game the following year.

But football was too popular a force to be kept out of the Tournament of Roses for long. In 1916 the game known today as "the Granddaddy of Them All" was reinstated, and in 1920 construction began on the Rose Bowl Stadium. The structure, which seats approximately a hundred thousand in its current configuration, originally featured fifty-seven thousand seats and opened for business in 1923. The stadium was initially financed by offering fans ten years' worth of tickets at a hundred dollars a pop. And they happily snapped them up.

The Rose Bowl celebrated its tenth consecutive year of New Year's Day play in 1926. Most of the previous matchups had been East-West pairings, featuring teams such as Yale, Harvard, Princeton, and Washington. This was designed to create as much intersectional rivalry and excitement as possible. Southern teams were not even considered prior to 1926, partly because there was a considerable bias, especially on the part of the West Coast organizers. Teams from the West (and East and Midwest) were believed to be superior to teams from the South.

In the early 1900s folks in the West, East, and Midwest had an elitist attitude in general. It's no secret there was bigotry directed toward southerners stemming from the Civil War. Many northerners looked down on the largely rural South and its relative poverty. They also looked down on their brand of football. Until Wallace Wade fielded a team that ultimately no one could fault (Bama was one of only three unbeaten teams in the country that year), southern teams never even thought about playing in Pasadena on New Year's Day.

All aboard! Bama's official party boards the train in Birmingham. Destination: Pasadena, California.

As people wrapped gifts and made eggnog to prepare to celebrate the holidays in late 1925, the Alabama football team packed their bags for the 2,013-mile train ride from Tuscaloosa to Pasadena to meet the University of Washington Huskies, veterans of the Rose Bowl. Just the trip itself was a big event for most of these players, many of whom had never before traveled out of the state.

The team boarded the train two weeks ahead of time. President Denny suggested the boys use their time during the four-day trip to study, but Coach Wade wanted their minds and bodies on football. On the train they studied playbooks. When the train made its scheduled stops, the team got off and did wind sprints. In Arizona, they even borrowed a high school practice field for a full scrimmage. When they arrived in Pasadena on Christmas Eve, Coach Wade called a practice for Christmas Day.

There was time for some fun, though. During the trip, the team saw the Grand Canyon. Once in California, the players met Hollywood movie stars and posed for pictures at tourist spots. But not for long. Fearing distractions would cause disaster, Coach Wade put a stop to the excitement, virtually sequestering his team in the hotel until game day—except for practice, of course.

No doubt the Bama players must have been incredibly excited. But they must have been reasonably anxious as well. The press back home was building up the game against Washington to be nothing less than a Civil War rematch. (Even though the state of Washington was not involved in that particular conflict.) The press out West and in other parts of the country heavily favored the Washington Huskies to say the least. The only edge reporters grudgingly gave to Alabama was regarding the weather—Bama was used to balmy game days while its opponent, the University of Washington, was probably not.

Bama was definitely the underdog. The Huskies were a fast, big, tough team who had gone unbeaten all season. (Only a tie with Nebraska marred their perfect record.) Sportswriters said the team from the Northwest had better tacklers and better runners. Many of their stories were written about the Huskies' all-American halfback George Wilson, who had made his name

Believe it or not, ball-carrier Johnny Mack Brown broke this one for a long gain.

Photo courtesy of the Paul W. Bryant Museum, the University of Alabama.

in his team's victory against Navy two years earlier. One story claimed that Wilson had recently turned down the then outrageous sum of $3,000 to turn pro. Part of the reason Wilson gave for his decision was a desire to help his team defeat Alabama.

When New Year's Day 1926 finally arrived, a crowd of forty-five-thousand-plus gathered to cheer the two teams. The Huskies kicked off and Bama completed a series of quick passes, landing them in touchdown range, right around the Washington fifteen yard line. Then, George Wilson intercepted a pass intended for Johnny Mack Brown and ran it all the way back to the forty-seven yard line. The Bama defenders were now officially awake.

On the next series, Washington scored. They missed the extra point but they led the game by six. It wasn't long before they scored again. Incredibly, though, they missed another extra point. Then the Huskies, up by twelve points, suffered a major setback when Wilson was knocked unconscious late in the second quarter by Alabama players who hit him hard. By some accounts the Bama players were frustrated at Wilson's ability to break their line. By other accounts, they were fighting mad at an unnecessarily rough cheap shot he made while tackling Johnny Mack Brown. Regardless, Wilson was temporarily out of the game.

During halftime, Coach Wade gathered his team together and said, "They told me boys from the South would fight." He then got specific, telling his quarterback, "Go ahead, Pooley. Give 'em everything you've got. Run the ball yourself all you want. It's rough and tough out there, but you can do it."

In the third quarter Hubert did as he was told. He carried on five successive plays and drove in for a touchdown. Bill Buckler kicked the extra point. It was good. There was hope. The score was Washington 12, Alabama 7.

On their next possession, Bama halfback Grant Gillis passed to Johnny Mack Brown, who snagged the ball at the twenty-five yard line and ran it in for a touchdown. The extra point was good, putting Bama ahead 14-12. Then, incredibly, just a few plays later, Washington fumbled at midfield. Alabama recovered, and, again, Hubert passed to Johnny Mack Brown, who ran twenty yards for the score. Even though Bama missed the extra point, the news was still good. The Tide was up 20-12.

Everything seemed to be coming up roses for Alabama, but things turned

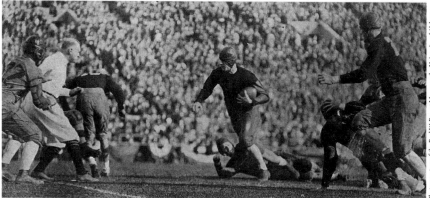

Photo courtesy of the Paul W. Bryant Museum, the University of Alabama.

Pooley Hubert goes off-tackle for a gain of 13 yards.

dicey when the Huskies put Wilson back in during the fourth quarter. He immediately ran for a gain of seventeen yards. The Huskies then pushed all the way to the Alabama thirty, setting up Wilson to pass to his quarterback, who took it in for another Huskie score. This time, Washington made its extra point. But it was not enough. Alabama won the game, 20-19.

It was a thrilling, amazing game. Years later, the nation's sportswriters, whose forebears had almost unanimously picked Washington to win, named the 1926 Rose Bowl one of the ten greatest college football games of all time.

Coach Wade was immediately bombarded with hundreds of telegrams congratulating him on his cluster of "firsts." First southern team to play in the Rose Bowl. First southern team to win it. Alabama's first trip to a bowl game. And of course, Alabama's first national title. (As of this writing, eleven more would follow.)

After the game, Wade spoke to reporters and gave credit where it was due: "I'll never forget my touchdown twins," he said. "Hubert, one of the greatest quarterbacks I've ever seen, and Brown, the kid with the hands of a magician."

Wade's "magician," Johnny Mack Brown, (aka "the Dothan Antelope") must have been profoundly inspired by his first visit to California. He would return to Hollywood after graduation and sign a contract with MGM Films. He made a career for himself as a movie cowboy, starring in some seventy films, including his breakout picture, *Billy the Kid*.

Many years later, when Coach Wade had plenty of perspective, not to mention two more national titles under his belt, he was still talking about New Year's Day. "I still regard the 1926 Alabama-Washington game as the most spectacular, exciting, and dramatic college football game in Alabama history."

Eighty years after that magnificent first Rose Bowl, we also have the benefit of perspective. We now know that there's nothing like Southern Football. Back in 1926 Alabama fans couldn't have been happier with their incredible team. As the squad returned home from California after their historic bowl appearance, they were cheered, paraded, and celebrated at every stop.

Some one thousand Tulane students turned out to cheer the Crimson Tide when they passed through New Orleans. William Little, the Alabama graduate credited with bringing football to the capstone, met them in Livingston, Alabama, and gave them gifts of turkeys and cakes. By the time the train reached Tuscaloosa, the whole town had already begun celebrating a festive holiday, complete with parades and parties for the players.

Photo courtesy of the Paul W. Bryant Museum, the University of Alabama.

All of Tuscaloosa turned out at the train depot to welcome the Rose Bowl champs home.

There was plenty to celebrate. Andrew Doyle, a Winthrop University professor who has written extensively about football, said: "You can look at the 1926 Rose Bowl as the most significant event in Southern Football history. What had come before was almost like a buildup, a preparation for this grand coming-out party. And it was a sublime tonic for southerners who were buffeted by a legacy of defeat, military defeat, a legacy of poverty, and a legacy of isolation from the American political and cultural mainstream."

Alabama fans now had a higher level of expectation for their team, which would continue for decades. Fans now expected their team to win. But could anyone have imagined, looking ahead to the 1926 season, that Bama would do it all over again?

Incredibly, despite the loss of senior stars Hubert and Brown, the Crimson

Tide went 9-0-1 in 1926. Again, they played in the Rose Bowl. This time they tied Stanford but still brought home the national championship for the second year in a row.

In 1947 the Tournament of Roses changed its guidelines and decided it would only invite teams from the Big Ten and the Pac-10 to compete in the Rose Bowl. For this reason, Alabama has not played in a Rose Bowl since 1946. But partially due to the spectacular Rose Bowl of 1926 and several thrillers that followed, the popularity of bowls exploded over the years. And Alabama has played in more than its fair share, chalking up a greedy number of Cotton Bowl, Sugar Bow, Liberty Bowl, and Orange Bowl wins during its storied history. In fact, The Crimson Tide has played in and won more bowls than any other college football program in the nation!

But 1926 started it all. It was the team that all future Alabama squads would compare themselves to. It was definitely the year of the Rose.

FIVE

Don Hutson

The End

OK, HERE GOES. THIS STATEMENT MAY GET ME IN TROUBLE, BUT I think the greatest player ever to wear the Crimson and White was quite possibly wide receiver Don Hutson. There have been dozens of incredible athletes to pass through the Capstone over the decades. But if we turn back the clock seventy years, we find a guy who set scores of college football records in his day. Certainly, he would still hold many of them today, if they had kept records back then as thoroughly as we do now. Since the SEC really didn't begin keeping good stats until 1937 or 1938, it's hard to do a big numbers comparison.

But no one can argue that Don Hutson created a brand new style of play and changed the offensive game forever. He was one of the best ever.

Don Hutson.

Photo courtesy of the Paul W. Bryant Museum, the University of Alabama.

I humbly submit that Hutson was the first true superstar in college football. True, legends such as Red Grange, George Gipp, and Jim Thorpe actually played before him. But only Hutson changed the way college football teams used the forward pass. Long after his amazing stint at Alabama, which he followed up with a stellar career as a pro with the Green Bay Packers, Hutson was named to *Sports Illustrated*'s Team of the Century.

There are so many things to say about Hutson, but probably the first thing that comes to mind regarding his college days is his performance during the 1935 Rose Bowl. Hutson had six receptions for 165 yards and two touchdowns in Bama's 29-13 win over Stanford. (The Rose Bowl Hall of Fame inducted him in 1993 for this performance.)

As incredible as this showing was, fans had come to expect such things of Hutson. He spoiled them. For Hutson, a two-touchdown day was almost run-of-the-mill.

Hutson's prowess on the football field was well documented. But not all Bama fans know that he was originally recruited as a baseball player and came to the University of Alabama on a partial baseball scholarship. He played and excelled in center field for the Tide. Incredibly, during his "off" time, he also ran and excelled at track.

An old story has it that Hutson wasn't even going to try out for the football team. However, a friend of his, Bob Seawall, a star on Hutson's high school team who was heavily recruited by Alabama football coaches, talked him into it. Ironically, Seawall dropped out of school after two years, and Hutson, who came out for the team as a walk-on, went on to become the star of the team.

Hutson's roommate and best friend at Alabama was none other than Paul W. "Bear" Bryant, a one-sport guy who also played end on the football team. Bryant was good, but Hutson was great, which explains why Bryant was nicknamed "The Other End."

Bryant and Hutson grew up near to each other in Arkansas and even played football on competing high school teams (Hutson in Pine Bluff,

Paul W. "Bear" Bryant in his playing days.

Photo courtesy of the Paul W. Bryant Museum, the University of Alabama.

Bryant in Moro Bottom). The funny thing was, though, Hutson didn't even play football until his senior year in high school. And even then, he was hardly a star. That would come later.

Bryant, who told many stories about Hutson over the years, spun a great one about his ex-roommate, the all-around athlete:

"The best story about Hutson is the one about his love for other sports," Bryant said. "Once during an Alabama baseball game, Hutson wore his track suit under his baseball flannels because a dual track meet was scheduled simultaneously on the track adjacent to the baseball diamond. Between innings, Don stripped off his baseball togs, got into the starting block, and ran the one-hundred-yard dash in 9.8 [seconds] to win the race."

But no doubt about it, Hutson is best remembered as a football player. He played on some incredible teams from 1932 to 1934, getting a little help from other standout players, including Bryant and the tremendous halfback Dixie Howell. But Coach Frank Thomas singled out Hutson and paid him the highest of compliments when he called Hutson "the best player I ever coached."

Don Hutson, USC Coach Howard Jones, Frank Thomas, and Dixie Howell.

Photo courtesy of the Paul W. Bryant Museum, the University of Alabama.

When Hutson first came out for the team, coaches were less than impressed with his 160-pound physique. In fact, Hutson didn't see much playing time until midway through his junior year. By that time he had gained some weight and, by some accounts, grew an inch or two, topping out at six-foot-one and 175 pounds. It wasn't about size, though. Once Hutson got the chance to play, he amazed everyone with his speed and agility.

"That was the big thing some people forget about Hutson," Bryant remembered. "The speed that propelled him beyond the defenders and enabled him to catch all those passes for us and for the Green Bay Packers when he played for them."

Logging all that time on the track (and as the legend goes, chasing snakes as a kid!) obviously paid off. Hutson was fast. Fast enough to get behind defenders and catch passes. Lots of them. He caught all these passes in such spectacular ways that he is often said to have changed the way college football teams viewed and used the forward pass. In fact, after considering his college and pro career in its entirety, the Pro Football Hall of Fame went so far as to credit him with inventing modern pass receiving, highlighting his "Z-outs, buttonhooks, hook-and-gos, and a whole catalog of moves and fakes."

It must have been a spectacular thing to see Hutson's inventions in the making.

As mentioned, Hutson didn't really get started until his senior year. When spring practice opened in 1934, Coach Frank Thomas layered his offense around the combination of Hutson,

Don Hutson

"I've got it!" And he didn't miss many.

Photo courtesy of the Paul W. Bryant Museum, the University of Alabama.

who had begun to show his explosive receiving talents, and Dixie Howell, who could pass—and kick—like nobody's business. Even Coach Thomas admitted later he had no idea what a truly amazing combination this would turn out to be.

The season began with a series of lopsided Bama victories. The Tide beat Howard, 24-0, Sewanee, 35-6, and Mississippi State, 41-0. Things really got exciting when, for the second year in a row, Bama beat Tennessee, 13-6.

The Other End and the End.

During this matchup, Hutson notably caught one pass to set up the first touchdown and then showed off his 9.8 speed when he scored the second touchdown on a short end-around run.

"You've beaten Tennessee," Coach Thomas said. "You can go all the way."

The coach's words turned out to be right on target. The Tide went on to pile up more lopsided victories, beating Georgia, 26-6, Kentucky, 24-14, and Clemson, 40-0. The recurring theme of all these wins? Howell hitting Hutson for pass after pass.

Bama ended the 1934 regular season at 9-0. After an incredible year, the Tide traveled to California to play Stanford in the Rose Bowl for the national championship.

The Tide got a huge scare early in the game, when Stanford recovered a Bama fumble and ran it in for a score. Winston Groom, author of *The Crimson Tide* (and that other little book, *Forrest Gump*), quotes humorist Will Rogers as saying this was a mistake on Stanford's part: "It just made Alabama mad. That first score was just like holding up a picture of Sherman's March to the Sea."

Whether they were mad as hell or just determined to win, the Tide rallied quickly and took the lead. But then Bama got another big scare when

CAPTAIN BILL LEE
All-American Tackle

MILLARD HOWELL
All-American Halfback

DON HUTSON
All-American End

Photo courtesy of the Paul W. Bryant Museum, the University of Alabama.

The 1934 championship season in review.

Photo courtesy of the Paul W. Bryant Museum, the University of Alabama.

Hutson: a Bama and Green Bay Packer great.

Dixie Howell reported stomach cramps. Thomas decided to let his passer rest and go with the run for a while. So, at the end of the first quarter, he sent Hutson into the huddle with instructions for the next set of plays.

In those days, according to Winston Groom, subs coming into a game could not speak inside the huddle until after the first play was over. So, when Joe Riley, Howell's replacement who was calling the play, saw Hutson enter the huddle he could only assume the coach wanted him to pass. Indeed, the words *Hutson* and *pass* had become pretty much linked at the elbow. So Riley, unwittingly against the coach's wishes, hurled a fifty-yard pass to Hutson, who made the catch on the fourteen yard line and ran it in for the score.

Coach Thomas went with the flow and resumed the passing game. Howell returned to the game in the second quarter. He and Hutson picked up where they left off and sealed the deal for the Tide before halftime even began by putting twenty-two points on the board.

(Ultimately, the Howell-Hutson combo came up with twenty-four of Bama's twenty-nine points.)

At the end of this particular New Year's Day, Hutson had logged six catches for two touchdowns, and Bama won the game, 29-13. To this day people consider this one of the greatest receiving performances in college football history.

As we've seen over the years, being a college football star does not guarantee a successful career in the pros. Think of all the Heisman Trophy winners who are never heard from again. That's in large part because NFL players as a whole are bigger, stronger, and faster—they play a different game from the collegiate version. Hutson was incredibly fast but compared to many NFL players, he was just average in size. (By today's standards, he was incredibly small. For that reason, some people doubted this talented guy would be able to make it in the pros. He proved them wrong.)

After graduating from the University of Alabama in 1935, the all-American and all-SEC Hutson was recruited by the Green Bay Packers and the Brooklyn Dodgers (the football team) to play pro football. According to the Pro Football Hall of Fame, somehow Hutson made a commitment to both teams, even going so far as to sign contracts with both organizations.

NFL president Joe Carr ruled on the matter and declared that the team whose contract had the earlier postmark would be honored. Thanks to a U.S. Postal Service stamp which showed the Packers' package had been sent seventeen minutes earlier than the envelope from Brooklyn, Green Bay had its new star.

Hutson was a perfect fit for the Packers' style of play. Green Bay, under Coach Curly Lambeau, was one of the few teams at the time known to be pass-friendly. (By the way, Brooklyn, where Hutson almost landed, was not.) Most teams ran the ball the majority of the time, saving passes, especially long bombs, as a last resort or a surprise move against a stronger opponent.

Hutson got busy catching passes for Green Bay right away. During the second game of his career, a matchup against the Chicago Bears, Packer quarterback Arnie Herber connected with Hutson on the very first play. The rookie star then ran it in to complete an eighty-three-yard pass play for a touchdown.

From the start it was apparent that Hutson was earning every penny of his then-lucrative $300 weekly salary. His pay was in fact so generous for that era that the Packers had to write him two checks of $150 each so he could draw on two different banks in Green Bay. (It was the depression and cash flow was sometimes limited, even at financial institutions.)

It is fairly well known that reporters didn't talk to players much in Hutson's day, which seemed to suit the humble Hutson just fine. But his coach, the legendary Curly Lambeau, evidently was at no loss for words when talking about his star receiver: "He would glide downfield, leaning forward as if to steady himself close to the ground," Lambeau said. "Then, as suddenly as you gulp or blink an eye, he would feint one way and go the other, reach up like a dancer, gracefully squeeze the ball, and leave the scene of this accident—the accident being the defensive backs who tangled their feet up and fell trying to cover him."

His fellow players, such as teammate Tony Canadeo, didn't seem to mind talking about Hutson, either. "He had all the moves," Canadeo said. "He invented the moves. And he had great hands and speed, deceptive speed. He could go get the long ones, run the hitch, the down-and-out. He'd go over the middle, too, and he was great at getting off the line because he always had people popping him."

Hutson played in Green Bay for eleven years. By the time he retired in 1945, he held eighteen NFL records. Some have been broken, some still stand. Hutson is perhaps best remembered for setting the mark for most career touchdown receptions (ninety-nine), an NFL record that stood for forty years until Steve Largent, the great receiver for Seattle, passed him in 1989 with his one hundredth touchdown catch. (Largent has since been passed by Cris Carter and then Jerry Rice.)

Speaking in 1989 Hutson talked about how he felt when his records were surpassed. "I love to see my records broken," Hutson said. "I really do. You get a chance to re-live a part of your life, the whole experience."

During his Green Bay days, Hutson led the league in receptions (eight times), in receiving yards (seven times), and in touchdown receptions (nine times). All these records remain intact.

Hutson was named All-Pro five times and twice won the Joe F. Carr Trophy as the NFL's most outstanding player. Of course, it wasn't all about individual achievement for Hutson: his team won the league championship three times during his career, in 1936, 1939, and 1944.

When talking about this man who many consider to be the greatest pass receiver who ever lived, it's tempting to make a long list of numbers just for "shock and awe." I mean, the man caught 488 passes in his career. The stats are just staggering.

Even though the occasional naysayer likes to note that Hutson played several of his best pro seasons from 1941 to 1945, when many young

American athletes were off fighting a war, we have to remember that Hutson set all those records in an era where teams played just ten to twelve games a season. There is no denying his consistency and display of sheer talent over his college and pro careers that spanned twenty-plus years. There is also no telling what kind of numbers an athlete like Hutson would have posted had he played a sixteen-game (or even a fourteen-game) season like teams of today do.

Quite simply, the man was one of a kind. In discussing Hutson, there's so much more to talk about than just his numbers. Like most players of his era, Hutson played both offense and defense. ("Yes, Johnny, we not only had to walk twenty miles in the snow to get to school, but we had to play both ways.") When he wasn't busy catching all those passes, he played a little defensive end. (During his final six seasons, he picked off some thirty passes.)

Hutson also moonlighted as a place kicker—he hit seven field goals and 172 extra points in his career! (Here come those numbers again: he held the record as Packers' all-time scoring leader with 823 points until Ryan Longwell pulled ahead of him in 2003.)

Imagine this guy executing a spectacular pass pattern, running it in for a touchdown, and staying on the field to boot the extra point. It boggles the mind.

With everything he accomplished, Hutson's most lasting legacy is the way he changed the offensive game. (Subsequently, teams had to react to these changes, so you can also say he changed the way defense is played as well!)

He is credited with inventing modern pass receiving. When Hutson began his pro career, few NFL teams employed forward passes. By the time he retired, all pro teams had forward passing in their game plans. In response to this new kind of football, teams began utilizing double coverage and triple-teaming—things that had been unheard of pre-Hutson.

It's easy to get bogged down in the encyclopedia-style explanation of Hutson's brand of football. But in the end, we have to go back to the fact that Hutson was a spectacular athlete. To put it simply, he was just really damn fast.

Dwight Sloan, who played defense against Hutson, confirms this fact: "I remember the first time I played against him. He came out for a pass and I had no trouble keeping up with him. *This isn't too hard*, I thought to myself, and then I couldn't find him. Suddenly, I looked behind me and he was far up the field reeling in the pass. He had shifted into high gear and left me standing there."

WHEN PEOPLE HEAR THE WORDS *ALABAMA* AND *GREEN BAY* IN THE same sentence, they usually think of Bart Starr, the famous Packer quarterback who starred in the legendary Ice Bowl. Starr was a great pro. (Oddly, he struggled at Alabama, playing backup quarterback almost his entire college career.) But when you're in Wisconsin and you head off the highway into Green Bay and drive onto Lombardi Avenue, there is a massive indoor practice facility directly across from Lambeau Field. The name emblazoned on the side? Don Hutson.

The Don Hutson Center is a gorgeous building, big enough not only to keep the Packers warm and dry during practice, but to park two jetliners inside. Hutson, eighty-one at the time, was there for the dedication of the structure in 1994. Considering all the Packer stars there have been over the years, it must have made Hutson incredibly proud to have his name chosen to grace this state-of-the-art facility. It certainly made Packers general manager Ron Wolf proud. "I don't know if there is such a thing as royalty in pro football," Wolf said. "But this (Don) is the closest I've ever come to it."

Hutson is a member of the Green Bay Packer Hall of Fame, of course. In 1951 he also became the first Packer player to have his number (14) retired. To date, he is one of only four players to receive this honor. (He was joined by Tony Canadeo in 1952, Bart Starr in 1973, and Ray Nitschke in 1983. Reggie White had his jersey, but not his number, retired in 1999.) Pretty impressive considering the caliber of players that followed Hutson onto Lambeau Field over the years.

As the years have passed, Hutson continued, and continues, adding to his long list of awards. He was a founding member of the NFL Hall of Fame. He was named to the NFL's All-Fifty-Year-Team, the NFL's All-Time Two-Way Team and the Seventy-fifth Anniversary Team. On June 26, 1997, at the age of eighty-four, Don Hutson passed away. But as long as anniversaries keep coming, he will be remembered.

Through his tremendous achievements, Don Hutson brought a great deal of attention and respect to the University of Alabama, long after he left Tuscaloosa. Bama fans were always happy to call this great player one of their own. They were—and still are—happy to say, "We knew him when . . ."

SIX

The Frank Thomas Era

Giving 110 Percent

IF THERE IS A PLACE ALMOST AS SYNONYMOUS WITH COLLEGE football as Alabama it would have to be Notre Dame. Between Touchdown Jesus, Knute Rockne, "the Gipper," and (more recently) "Rudy," Notre Dame has a rich tradition under its belt.

Imagine a man who played quarterback for legendary Notre Dame coach Knute Rockne, roomed with the Gipper (of "Win one for the Gipper" fame), and went on to have unimagined success as head coach at the University of Alabama. Now there's a guy with some kind of football pedigree. Of course we're talking about Frank Thomas.

Coach Frank Thomas.

Thomas came to Alabama as head coach in 1931 to succeed the incredibly successful Wallace Wade, who had taken the Crimson Tide to unparalleled heights and done no less than establish the winning tradition that the football program still savors to this day.

Wade left a winning legacy at Alabama. To ensure that it lasted, he recommended his successor to President Denny when he resigned.

Photo courtesy of the Paul W. Bryant Museum, the University of Alabama.

"There's a young backfield coach at Georgia who should become one of the greatest coaches in our nation," Wade said. "He played football under Knute Rockne at Notre Dame, and Rockne called him one of the smartest players he ever coached. His name is Frank Thomas, and I don't believe you could pick a better man."

Indeed, Rockne himself had indirectly given Thomas his endorsement years earlier when Thomas was still a star senior player at Notre Dame.

"It's amazing how much football sense that Thomas kid has," Rockne told a reporter. "He can't miss becoming a great coach someday."

So, it was decided: Thomas was the man. Wade himself called Thomas to let him know Bama would be calling. Then, in July 1930, Thomas traveled to Birmingham, full of high hopes mixed with his fair share of apprehension, to meet with Dr. Denny. He was a little shocked by the less-than-warm-and-fuzzy atmosphere in the meeting with his new employer.

Thomas' 16-year record at Alabama: 115-24-7.

Photo courtesy of the Paul W. Bryant Museum, the University of Alabama.

"Mr. Thomas," Denny said, "now that you have accepted our proposition, I will give you the benefit of my views, based on many years of observation. It is my conviction that material is 90 percent, coaching ability 10 percent. I desire further to say that you will be held to strict accounting for delivering the remaining 10 percent."

Atlanta reporter Ed Camp, who attended the meeting with Thomas, remembered Thomas's reaction. "Those were the hardest and coldest words I have ever heard," Thomas said. "Do you reckon his figures are right?"

"I think the proportion was considerably off," Camp said. "But there is no doubt the good doctor means what he says."

As we now know, Thomas would give much more than his fair 10 percent in the years that followed. In fact, few would argue that Thomas probably contributed more like 110 percent. From 1931 to 1946, he became Alabama's most successful coach to that point, piling up a gaudy record of 115 wins, twenty-four losses, and seven ties. His teams brought home two national championships to Tuscaloosa. Indeed, handing the baton off to Thomas turned out to be a very good call.

FRANK WILLIAM THOMAS, THE YOUNGEST OF SIX CHILDREN, WAS born November 15, 1898, in Muncie, Indiana. His parents were iron-working Welsh immigrants. When he was ten, they moved the family to East Chicago, where Frank later became the first four-sport letterman at Washington High School. One of those sports was football, of course.

Young Frank "Tommy" Thomas was offered a scholarship to Western State College in Kalamazoo. In his first football game there, the 135-pound Thomas ran eighty-seven yards for a touchdown. With the help of an alum with a talent for spotting good football players, Tommy transferred to Notre Dame and played quarterback for coach Knute Rockne his junior and senior years.

It was in Notre Dame's undefeated season of 1920 that Thomas roomed with George Gipp, the great Notre Dame all-American player

Photo courtesy of the Paul W. Bryant Museum, the University of Alabama.

Thomas: the Gipper's roommate at Notre Dame.

who scored eighty-three touchdowns on offense and allowed virtually no passes to be completed on his watch while playing defense. During his senior year at Notre Dame, Gipp contracted a serious throat infection and tragically died a few weeks later.

While he lay in his hospital bed, Gipper told Coach Rockne, "Sometime, Rock, when the team is up against it, when things are wrong and the breaks are beating the boys—tell them to go in there with all they've got and win just one for the Gipper. I don't know where I'll be then, Rock, but I'll know about it and I'll be happy."

Evidently, Rockne called on the Gipper in a legendary pep talk some eight years later. (It worked. Notre Dame won.) Years later, Ronald Reagan starred as Gipp in the 1940 movie *Knute Rockne: All-American*.

Here's an interesting bit of trivia: When Alabama played in the Rose Bowl in 1938, a young sports reporter named Ronald Reagan spent a great deal of time interviewing the Alabama players and was reportedly quite enamored with their coach, Frank Thomas. Perhaps it was here that Reagan got the inspiration he needed for the role of "the Gipper" which he would play two years later.

Having to digest the incredible sadness of Gipp's death alongside the great happiness of his team's success on the football field, Thomas graduated from

Frank Thomas (right) accepting a football from Wade Wallace.

Photo courtesy of the Paul W. Bryant Museum, the University of Alabama.

Notre Dame in 1922. He immediately got busy fulfilling Rockne's prophecy that he would become a great coach when he accepted a job coaching the backfield for University of Georgia coach Kid Woodruff. Thomas gladly accepted his paycheck of $2,500 a year and helped Georgia win all but two games (against Yale and Alabama) in 1923. When Harry Mehre was named head coach, Thomas was promoted and became his assistant. A few years later, Alabama came calling.

After accepting Dr. Denny's offer, Thomas attended the 1930 Rose Bowl and witnessed the glorious Alabama victory that capped Wade's incredible final season. Thomas even traveled back to Alabama with Wade and his team, so as to get better acquainted with his players. (Historical note: author Clyde Bolton reports that while Thomas was in Pasadena, his son, Frank Jr., was being born back in Georgia. Now that's an understanding wife.)

Harry Gilmer (#52), Coach Thomas and Vaughn Mancha (#41).

His first year at Alabama was a stiff challenge for Thomas. Coach Wallace Wade wasn't only a hard act to follow—he was an impossible act to follow. For one thing, most of the starters had graduated. Thomas had to virtually start over. He knew in order to survive, let alone win, he would have to establish his own brand of coaching right away.

Wade had garnered a great deal of success with his approach, mainly, the single-wingback formations. But they say you should do what you know, so

Thomas brought in the Notre Dame box formation. The team took to the new offense right away—it just worked, whether you were doing it for the Gipper or not.

In his first outing as head coach, Thomas' Crimson Tide clobbered their first opponent, Howard, 42-0. This was a sign of many good things to come. Often utilizing the talents of fullback and punter Johnny Cain, one of the few starters returning from the previously perfect season, Bama managed to finish the season 9-1 and outscore its opponents, 370-57.

The next season, 1932, was another one to make Bama fans proud of their new coach: The Tide went 8-2, losing close games to Tennessee (7-3) and Georgia Tech (6-0).

The old Southern Conference was divided up in 1933. From now on, Bama would be part of a new conference, the Southeastern Conference (SEC). In another sign of things to come, Alabama won the SEC title that year as they finished 7-1-1. (They would go on to make the SEC title their own, winning it twenty-one times to date. The only schools who come close to Bama's tally are Tennessee, with thirteen, and Georgia, with eleven.)

Then came the incredible, spectacular, unbeatable year of 1934. In just his third year as head coach, Frank Thomas led his team to a perfect 10-0 season. The Crimson Tide was named SEC champs. After beating Stanford in the Rose Bowl, they were crowned national champs.

Thomas had made it look so easy. But he gave plenty of credit to his incredible players that season, going out on a limb and calling them the best team he ever coached. What a pack of talent!

The superstars of this team were receiver Don Hutson and fullback Dixie Howell. Together, the two were an unstoppable scoring machine, both setting innumerable college records. They are probably best known for teaming up at the 1934 Rose Bowl. Between the two of them, they accounted for twenty-four of the twenty-nine points Bama scored in its 29-13 victory over Stanford.

Don Hutson's roommate on that team was none other than "the Other End," Paul W. "Bear" Bryant. Bryant was an outstanding, tough player known for his excellent blocking and consistent execution. He was only overshadowed by the fact that Hutson was such an amazing, innovative player—the first real star receiver in college football. But Bryant distinguished himself in many ways, notably by playing with a broken leg during a game against Tennessee.

There was probably just one man, in Bear's opinion, who could inspire a player to do such a thing. That man was Frank Thomas.

"You sure that helmet's gonna hold up?"

"Coach Bryant's hero was Frank Thomas," confirmed Harry Gilmer, another star who played for Thomas a few years after Bryant. "He was his coach. He really listened and looked up to him."

When Bryant came to Alabama as a player in 1932, he was instantly impressed with Thomas, mainly because of his Notre Dame credentials.

During his first year Bryant was a red-shirted freshman who attended practice while finishing up classes at Tuscaloosa High in order to get enough credits to begin his college courses.

According to Bryant biographer Mickey Herskowitz, one day the Bama varsity players were having a hard time blocking a punt. Thomas pointed over to Bryant and said, "Let this little high school boy show you how."

Bryant stepped in, brushed aside an end with a forearm, and threw himself at the kicker. Both the ball and the kicker were flattened. Bear then returned to his place with the other redshirts.

Thomas had given him praise, and Bryant rose to the challenge. Bryant knew he had curried favor with Thomas. He also took away a lesson he would use as a coach with his own players years later.

It wasn't the only time Thomas used positive reinforcement to get the best from his players. Years later, Bryant told a story about going to the Rose Bowl in 1935:

> I remember everything about it," Bryant said. "We were on the train, and Coach Thomas was talking to three coaches and Red Heard, the athletic director at LSU. Coach Thomas said, 'Red, this is my best football player. This is the best player on my team.' Well, shoot, I could have gone right out on top. He was getting me ready. And I was, too. I would have gone out there and killed myself for Alabama that day.

Years later, when Paul Bryant, the player, became Bear Bryant, the coach (first, an assistant coach for Thomas, later a head coach), he brought with

Harry Gilmer, Coach Thomas and Vaughn Mancha ponder their bowl possibilities.

Photo courtesy of the Paul W. Bryant Museum, the University of Alabama.

him the lessons he learned from Coach Thomas. Bryant also often returned to the source.

"When Bryant was head coach at Kentucky, there was never a week that he didn't call Thomas and talk over strategies," Harry Gilmer said. "This was the guy Bryant talked to about problems that would come up with his team."

Bryant's longtime radio producer, Bert Bank, also remembers Bryant asking for a little help from his hero.

"When he was coaching at Kentucky, Bryant would slip down to Alabama when nobody knew it and talk to Thomas about the game coming up," Bank said. "He said Coach Thomas knew more about figuring out the offense and the defense than any coach he'd ever known. He was a great strategist."

It went beyond just coaching, though.

"I remember every time I saw Coach Bryant, he would ask me how Coach Thomas was doing," Gilmer said. "So all of us have our heroes. Even as tough as Bryant was, he had his, too."

What was it that Bryant found so admirable about Frank Thomas? Bryant's longtime assistant coach, Clem Gryska, who also played for Thomas, explained it this way: "Coach Bryant had a lot of respect for Coach Thomas because he was so sharp. He was intelligent and very low key. He was very demanding but in a subtle way. If you made a mistake, he'd say, 'Let's do it correctly,' instead of jerking you out and putting someone else in."

Frank Thomas continued layering his proverbial cake of winning seasons. The 1935 team went 6-2-1 in what was a building season after the losses of Hutson, Howell, and company.

In 1936 they bettered themselves by going undefeated (8-0-1). In 1937 Bama again won the SEC title, finishing the regular season 9-1 before losing to California in the Rose Bowl.

Bama marked a milestone in 1940 when it played its first night game, that coming against Spring Hill College at Mobile's Murphy High Stadium. Then, in 1941, Thomas notched his second national championship when Bama beat Texas A&M 9-2, topping the year off with a victory in its first visit to the Cotton Bowl.

Everything changed in 1942, not just for Alabama football but for all of the country when the United States entered World War II. It must have been difficult for Thomas and his players as they wondered, *Was it appropriate to keep playing football when brothers and fathers were away at war? Or was it their duty to keep people's spirits up back home?*

They did their best. In 1942 Bama played several teams made up of college all-stars stationed at military bases. A year later Coach Thomas did his best to put together a team, but there simply weren't enough players (let alone opponents to play). So, in 1943 Bama took a year off from football.

In 1944 Thomas managed to put together a most varied and unusual team of only twenty players. These included men who weren't qualified for the service for medical reasons, as well as some returning vets. The rest of the team was made up of very young freshmen, whom Thomas dubbed "War Babies." One freshman, a player Thomas had scouted during his downtime in 1943, was a tailback from Woodlawn High School in Birmingham. His name: Harry Gilmer.

Photo courtesy of the Paul W. Bryant Museum, the University of Alabama.

"Just go long. Harry will get it to ya."

During the opening game of 1944, Gilmer, all 157 pounds of him, ran back a kickoff for ninety-five yards and a thrilling touchdown. Bama tied LSU, 27-27, that day. But all eyes were on Gilmer. And the best was yet to come.

When the 1945 season rolled around, the war was over. Bama celebrated with a perfect 10-0 season and a trip to the Rose Bowl. Bama was absolutely whipping its opponents, the USC Trojans (they were up, 34-0, in the fourth quarter), when Thomas put in his second string.

Coach Thomas showed his compassionate side by putting one particular player into the game. Nick Terlizzi was sitting on the bench with a broken leg when Coach Thomas asked, "Nick, would you like to say you have played in the Rose Bowl?" Terlizzi answered, "Yes, sir, coach!"

"Well, go out there, but don't get in any mix-ups and get hurt," Thomas said. "Stay out of the way of all the plays."

Thomas earned USC Coach Jeff Cravath's respect by putting in his backup players and not running up the score.

"There goes a great man," Cravath said. "I'll never forget what he did today. If he wanted to, he could have named the score."

Coach Malcomb Laney, Coach Frank Thomas and Joe Kilgrow, Sugar Bowl 1945.

Photo courtesy of the Paul W. Bryant Museum, the University of Alabama.

Bama won it, 34-14. The win was bittersweet, however, in that it was the last time a southern team would be invited to the Rose Bowl. That year the committee decided from then on to include only teams from the Big Ten and Pac-10.

The incredible Frank Thomas was head coach at Alabama from 1931-1946

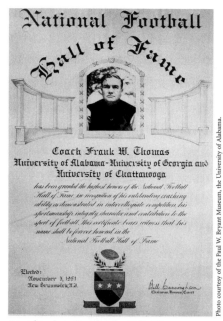

Coach Frank W. Thomas
University of Alabama-University of Georgia and
University of Chattanooga

has been granted the highest honors of the National Football
Hall of Fame in recognition of his outstanding coaching
ability as demonstrated in intercollegiate competition, his
sportsmanship, integrity, character and contribution to the
sport of football. This certificate bears witness that his
name shall be forever honored in the
National Football Hall of Fame

Elected:
November 3, 1951
New Brunswick, N.J.

Bill Cunningham
Chairman, Honors Court

Bama fans always knew he was a Hall of Famer.

Photo courtesy of the Paul W. Bryant Museum, the University of Alabama.

where in sixteen seasons he won 115, lost 24, and tied 7. Fans and players wanted Coach Thomas to stay on forever, but, sadly, he was forced to retire due to health reasons, primarily a heart condition coupled with high blood pressure. Players were not surprised by his retirement; evidently he spent his last year as coach commanding his team from a chair on an elevated trailer and speaking in a labored voice through a bullhorn.

Several years after his retirement, Thomas, despite being in very ill health, attended the Homecoming game of 1953. Leaning on the arm of his son, Frank Jr., Thomas walked onto the field at Denny Stadium and received a replica of his Football Hall of Fame Award. He told the crowd, "Friends, this is the happiest day of my life."

A bittersweet ending. Thomas passed away in Tuscaloosa in 1954. But it's the strong, stocky midwesterner who people in Alabama remember. The tough guy with a brilliant mind and a bit of a soft side. We remember the winner.

SEVEN

Harry Gilmer
Taking the Leap

OPEN UP A BOOK OF ALABAMA FOOTBALL STATISTICS OR CLICK "records" on the terrific Web site www.rolltide.com, scroll through the list, and you will be virtually blinded by one name popping up over and over again: Harry Gilmer.

Harry Gilmer.

Harry Gilmer was absolutely the star of his era and arguably the best all-around, four-year player Bama has ever had. During his time at Alabama, (1944–47), Gilmer recorded fifty-two career touchdowns—still a Bama record. He was named player of the year and Rose Bowl MVP in 1945.

In those days players played both offense and defense, so Gilmer's records litter both sides of the board. In 1946, he led the team in passing, rushing, interceptions, punt returns, and kickoff returns. The list of his achievements runs for pages and pages.

Gilmer was best known for his leaping style of passing. He would take the snap, step back, jump up, then throw the ball because he was small and couldn't see over the huge linemen! I mean he would jump high in the air, then send the ball sailing downfield! Just incredible!

He developed this technique when he played sandlot ball as a kid. He was small even then. When Gilmer got to college, he still was comparatively smaller than the other guys. But he was prepared. He had perfected his flying leap.

Here was this little tailback who played for Woodlawn High School in

Gilmer: a star from the start.

Photo courtesy of the Paul W. Bryant Museum, the University of Alabama.

Birmingham. Coach Frank Thomas was told to keep an eye on the young man. Thomas did just that, and after convincing Gilmer to come to Alabama, the 155-pound jack-of-all-gridiron-trades made Bama history.

Gilmer was born in 1926, a year that allowed him to just miss being old enough for the draft in World War II. When he was still a high school star, many schools recruited Gilmer, but Bama won the day.

According to author Clyde Bolton in his book, *The Crimson Tide: A Story of Alabama Football*, when Gilmer arrived on campus, he was suffering from an ulcer. He was placed on a strict diet of milk, cereal, and strained vegetables—good for the stomach but not so good for building the bulk needed in a football player.

Nonetheless, Gilmer made up his mind to play. There would be no stopping him. Normally, freshmen do not play their first year in college football. Even when they are as talented as Gilmer. But this was wartime. After not being able to field a team in 1943 because so many players were in the service, Thomas managed to put together a ramshackle squad of just twenty players in 1944. That year, the Crimson Tide was made up of returning vets, 4-F students (who weren't drafted for medical reasons), and a few freshmen Thomas called "War Babies." Gilmer led the pack.

Starting with the 1944 season opener against LSU, Gilmer made it clear to everyone that he was something special. He stunned the crowd by immediately returning a kickoff for an exciting ninety-five-yard touchdown. Bama tied that game, 27-27. But they had a new star on their hands and the coach, the fans, and his nineteen teammates knew it.

Coach Clem Gryska, who played with Gilmer in 1947, says Harry ruled the field from that very first game and never stopped the whole time he played at Alabama.

Part of Bama's 1947 team: (from bottom left): E. Salem, H. Gilmer, H. Morrow, G. Pettus, D. Kizzire, T. Whitley, V. Mancha, B. Chambliss, and M. Mizerany.

Photo courtesy of the Paul W. Bryant Museum, the University of Alabama.

"He was a gifted athlete who really carried the whole team," Gryska said. "If you'd just stay out of his way, he'd move the ball down the field. He'd either run it, throw it, or kick it!"

A passing style all his own.

Photo courtesy of the Paul W. Bryant Museum, the University of Alabama.

Bama finished the 1944 season just 5-1-2 that year. Nonetheless, at season's end, the Tide received a Sugar Bowl bid to meet a powerful Duke team. They were mismatched to be sure (the Duke team was packed full of navy trainees). But Gilmer got a chance to show his stuff in front of a huge, seventy-thousand-plus crowd. He ran, he kicked, he passed. One pass in particular still has a special place in Bama lore. In the second quarter, Gilmer tripped over one Duke player. Two others had a piece of him when, suddenly, he broke loose for an instant, leapt high off the ground, and whipped the ball forty-one yards to Ralph Jones. The game was close but Duke prevailed, 29-26.

Even though Bama didn't win that Sugar Bowl, the team was able to leave town with heads held high. And Gilmer left town with a particularly impressive press clipping when sportswriter Grantland Rice said he was, "the greatest college passer I ever saw."

There were a lot of things to be optimistic about in 1945. The war was over and Bama football was back to full strength. The team had returned to a full squad—sixty guys. Again, though, it was an odd makeup of players. You had the War Babies (Gilmer, center Vaughn Mancha, etc.), who were sophomores now. You still had a few 4-F holdovers, plus a few more new freshmen. But now you also had some returning vets, some who were twenty-two and older, who had returned from the war to finish their education. In other words you had some seventeen-year-old guys who'd never stepped foot outside of Alabama, alongside toughened up war vets, some who had spent years overseas. And they were playing football together!

Somehow it worked.

"The older guys were nice to us; in fact, they were compassionate," Clem Gryska said. "I think they were very glad to be back and out of the service. They could see the youth in the other players and they kind of adopted us."

Somehow this team really meshed. They went 10-0 that year.

Coach Thomas got the players practicing right away, morning through afternoons, to whip them into shape as a team. No doubt these practices were actually fun for the army guys. But they had to learn to work together.

Bama opened the 1945 season by clobbering the Keesler Field Flyers, 21-0. (All three touchdowns were scored by Lowell Tew, another War Baby.)

Then, the Tide headed to Baton Rouge for a battle against LSU. This game was a high-flying event—literally. All eyes were in the air as the leaping Gilmer completed eight of sixteen passes for 188 yards and three touchdowns.

Next, Bama completely shut down South Carolina, 55-0, and then trounced Tennessee, 25-7.

The toughest game for the Tide that year came against Georgia, which boasted a "triple threat" player in the same mold as Gilmer, a guy named Charley Trippi. But Gilmer came through again, passing for three touchdowns, putting Bama over the top, 28-14.

The Tide was definitely on a roll and it simply refused to stop. They went on to win four more lopsided victories: against Kentucky (60-19), Vanderbilt (71-0), Pensacola (55-6), and Mississippi State (55-13).

Bama ended the regular season of 1945 with a perfect 9-0 record. Appropriately for that year, Army had the other best team in the nation and was the only team standing in the way of Bama's national championship. In fact, the Associated Press did name Army national champs. Army was stout that season. Doc Blanchard won the Heisman in 1945, his junior year. (He was the first junior to win the trophy.) His nineteen touchdowns and 115 total points led the Cadets to their undefeated season. Glenn Davis, who would eventually leave West Point as their all-time scoring leader, was also running rampant. These two men were coached by the legendary Earl "Red" Blaik, who won back-to-back championships at West Point in 1945 and 1946. But Bama kept its eye on the rose as they traveled to Pasadena for their sixth Rose Bowl Game, another matchup against USC.

Photo courtesy of the Paul W. Bryant Museum, the University of Alabama.

Smiles abound for Mancha and Gilmer.

The Tide had a few obstacles to overcome before they boarded the train west. The weather in Tuscaloosa was nasty, rainy, icy, and cold—making practices difficult. Plus, a flu epidemic was making the rounds, hitting players and coaches alike.

According to the author Clyde Bolton even assistant coach Happy Campbell had to remain in his Pullman berth during the entire train ride to Pasadena but refused to lose his sense of humor saying, "I'm going to fight this flu germ lying down."

The train was sixteen hours late in reaching its destination, but, finally, Alabama arrived in California. They were a bit bedraggled but had a few days to recover. Plus a few writers (but by no means the West Coast ones) even favored Bama to win.

No doubt USC was well aware of Bama's strengths, namely Gilmer's passing prowess. For that reason, Coach Thomas decided to throw the Trojans off the scent by switching the game plan a bit.

"We were supposed to get knocked off that day against Southern California," Gilmer said, "and they were all set to defense our passing attack. So Coach Thomas told us to stick to the running game and we had them completely baffled."

The tone of this Rose Bowl was set immediately when, early on, Trojan halfback Bobby Morris fumbled an Alabama punt on the USC seventeen yard line and Bama recovered. Gilmer then carried the ball three times, setting up Hal Self, who took it in for the score.

By the third quarter, the Tide had surged ahead, 27-0. Incredibly, at that point, USC had not made a single first down. Coach Thomas saw that the lead was secure and proceeded at some point to send in every player on the team, even the third-stringers.

Gilmer threw "only" fourteen times, but one of his passes connected with Hal Self for a touchdown. Mostly, he followed Coach Thomas's altered game plan and ran the ball, carrying it himself for 116 yards.

Bama won, 34-14. In the final tally, the Tide had gained an impressive 351 yards versus just forty-one yards for USC. Bama had piled up more points in this one game than all of the Trojans' previous eight Rose Bowl opponents combined.

ALL-AMERICAN
1945
Alabama Half
a passer second
to NONE

Indeed a passer second to none.

Photo courtesy of the Paul W. Bryant Museum, the University of Alabama.

This Rose Bowl victory would be the last for the Crimson Tide, since after that year, the committee decided to invite only Pac-10 and Big Ten teams in the future. If the Rose Bowl of 1946 had to be the last, at least Bama went out on top. Harry Gilmer was named Rose Bowl MVP. Though they missed being named national champs officially, they certainly felt as though they were. They were SEC champs, at least. They could not have had a better season. So, The Crimson Tide boarded the train to Tuscaloosa to celebrate mightily.

That 1945 team set a school record by scoring 430 points. Gilmer played a big part in that record and was named an all-American. He was also named Most Valuable Player of the SEC. He had plenty to brag about. But he didn't.

"He was very humble," Gryska said. "He was very low key and treated everyone really well. He was a grown-up. In fact, he was the only member of the squad who was married. Back then the coaches didn't want you to get married. But he was, and for lack of a better word, he was like a granddaddy to us. If we had a bad practice or got hurt, especially the younger players, he'd always come out and put his arm around you."

Maybe when you're that good, there's no need to talk about it. But we all know that many people do. Gilmer seems very much at ease with his incredible accomplishments, even to this day.

A few years back I hosted the taping of a terrific DVD, *The Alabama Football Legends Reunion*. There were so many great names in that room it was mind boggling—Ken Stabler, Jay Barker, Marty Lyons, Lee Roy Jordan, and Barry Krauss, just to name a few. And there was Harry Gilmer, kicking back comfortably in his cowboy boots, looking lean and small next to big men like Bob Baumhower and Dwight Stephenson. But they all wanted to hear what he had to say. He was the player they wanted to meet and listen to, and man, does he have great stories.

Just think of the things he's done and seen. He was on the airplane the first time the Alabama football team flew to a game, which was back in 1946. Here's how Gilmer remembered it:

We were going up to play Boston College. The airplanes were something like C-47s. And they wouldn't carry a full team. So there were a couple of them.

Well, we had this tackle on both offense and defense, Charlie Compton, who was a very, very good player. He was a very intense person—a war hero. We thought he was a little wacky. This guy didn't have an ounce of fat on his body. He was the leanest, best-conditioned athlete you have ever seen in your life. In the service, he supposedly volunteered to pull a string of small boats tied together to move some troops across a river. Something happened and the boats turned loose. So, in the shallow part of the river, he rounds up the boats, ties them back together and hangs onto them over his shoulder and starts walking up close to the bank so he can touch the bottom. He's under fire. They are shooting at him.

So, he winds up getting all kinds of medals and awards. Then, after getting out of the army he comes back to school and plays out his senior year with us.

We had just had an undefeated season the year before. We thought we were a pretty good team, then here comes this stud, man, I'm telling you! He really looked the part.

Anyway, he heard the coach announce that this would be the team's first trip on an airplane. After the meeting he goes up to Coach Thomas. And nobody really just walked up to Coach Thomas and started talking, but he did. He says, "Coach, I don't fly." The Coach says, "What do you mean you don't fly?" He says, "Well, I don't ride in airplanes."

Coach Thomas tells him this is the first time a team ever had a chance to ride in an airplane. Compton says, "I don't fly, so you better let me get on a train Wednesday so I will be there when you all get there." Coach Thomas says, "We can't have you splitting off away from the team like that." Compton says, "Well, I don't know what we're going to do. I don't fly."

Then Coach Thomas says, "Well, let's think about this. You were a brave guy in the service and got all those honors. What if we gave you a parachute? You wouldn't hesitate to jump out, right?" Compton said, "No." So Coach says, "Well, we will give you a chute and you don't even have to wear it where the others can see it. You can slide it under your seat. If there is some trouble, you can get that chute and put it on."

Compton looks up and says, "I'm not going to do it." Coach Thomas says, "I don't understand. You're brave enough. You could handle that."

Compton says, "No. I know that as soon as this plane got in trouble you would come running to me and say, 'Get that chute and give it to Gilmer!'"

Compton was the ultimate paradox. Here's this tough-as-nails guy. As the legend goes, he once gashed his cheek during a play and proceeded to sew it up himself, right on the sidelines, so he could go back in and play. Then, one game he refused to go in because he had a charley horse. Go figure.

Clem Gryska tells another story about their colorful teammate:

During one game, Charlie comes off the field and asks the manager to give him a pair of pliers. Back then we had cleats that you could tighten or change with pliers. We all thought he was going to make an equipment change or something. But he took those pliers and pulled his damn tooth out! No sedative or nothing!

With all this going on, who even thought to brag about making a few touchdowns?

The 1946 season was the last for Coach Thomas. His health (heart and blood pressure, mainly) was very poor. In fact, doctors and even the university president had been encouraging him to retire for some time. But he finished out the year. Again, his team was led by Harry Gilmer, who was the best passer in the nation and still just a junior! The Tide went 7-4 that year.

Gilmer and Mancha catch a breather.

In 1947 Gilmer and his teammates had a new coach, Red Drew. They went 8-3 and made a trip to the Sugar Bowl on New Year's Day. Unfortunately, their opponent, Texas, came away with the win that year. But nothing could take away from Gilmer's astonishing pile of accomplishments.

After he graduated, Gilmer was selected No. 1 overall in the NFL Draft by the Washington Redskins. He played six seasons in our nation's capital and went to two Pro Bowls for the 'Skins. He then finished up his pro career playing two seasons for the Detroit Lions.

Gilmer later became a head coach for the Lions, which made him the only player selected No. 1 in the draft as a player to later become a head coach for an NFL team.

But people in Alabama will always think of Harry Gilmer as a college star. No one in Alabama will ever forget him and his giant leaps.

EIGHT

The Bear Comes to Bama—1957

Mama Called

ON DECEMBER 3, 1957, IT WAS ANNOUNCED THAT PAUL "BEAR" Bryant would be the new head football coach at Alabama. At the time, Dwight Eisenhower was president, Elvis was in the army, and Bryant was a highly successful head coach at Texas A&M, where his team was in contention for the national championship. Prior to his four years in College Station, he had notched successful seasons as head coach at Maryland and Kentucky. Plus, he was a former Alabama football star and former Alabama assistant coach under Frank Thomas. He was family. And now he was returning home.

"Thank you, Mr. President."

Photo courtesy of the Paul W. Bryant Museum, the University of Alabama.

In his famous speech at the Shamrock Hotel in Houston, Coach Bryant, a self-described "Mama's Boy," explained his decision. The speech was a much longer version of the sound bite he would later repeat many times: "I left Texas A&M because my school called me. Mama called, and when Mama calls, then you just have to come running."

Case closed. The Texas A&M Aggies may not have been happy

about his leaving (there were still six years left on his contract), but Coach Bryant felt he had no choice. The university—his university—was in trouble. Mama called. She needed Coach Bryant. So he headed home.

The years prior to Bryant's return had been the worst imaginable for Alabama football fans. During his predecessor J. B. "Ears" Whitworth's tenure as head coach, Alabama had won a total of only four games in three years. For fans accustomed to national championships and trips to the Rose Bowl, this was unbelievable. And devastating.

By all accounts, Coach Whitworth, a former Alabama lineman, was a nice guy who was put into an impossible situation. The football program had already been in a declining mode when Coach Whitworth left his position as head coach at Oklahoma A&M to come to Alabama in 1955. The downslide began with the retirement of the enormously successful Frank Thomas in 1947. Harold "Red" Drew succeeded Thomas and stayed at the helm for eight seasons. Coach Drew won fifty-four, lost twenty-eight, and tied seven. Respectable, if not exactly national championship worthy, numbers. But 1954 was an exceptionally bad year, as Bama won four, lost five, and tied two. Especially painful was the season finale against Auburn—the Tigers shut out the Tide 28-0.

For Coach Whitworth, inheriting a dispirited team was difficult enough. But worse for him was the fact that he was hobbled by the administration. He was allowed to hire only two coaches of his choosing. He was not given an adequate budget for uniforms and equipment. Plus, athletic director Hank Crisp was also his defensive coach, which, according to press reports, made it difficult if not impossible to determine "who's in charge here."

Practices under Coach Whitworth were inconsistent—sometimes overly regimented, sometimes way too easy. The players also failed to become a cohesive unit, partially due to the fact that there was an enormous age disparity between eighteen-year-old freshmen and some of the juniors and seniors who had returned to school after serving in the Korean War.

There were a myriad of reasons why. But the bottom line was that things were *bad*. In 1955 the Tide lost every game. Three years in a row Bama failed to score against Tennessee even once! It was time to gain back Bama's earlier prominence. And many people thought they had just the man for the job: Paul W. Bryant.

A vision for the ages.

Photo courtesy of the Paul W. Bryant Museum, the University of Alabama.

Not everybody knows that Bryant was actually offered the Alabama head coaching job twice before 1957. In his book about the 1958 season, *Turnaround*, author Tom Stoddard says that Frank Thomas offered Bryant the job when he retired and that Bryant informally accepted, but the president of the University of Kentucky refused to let him out of his contract. Then in 1954, according to Bryant, he was offered the head coaching position again but turned it down due to concerns about splitting authority with athletic director Crisp and being perceived as pushing out Coach Drew, whom he knew and respected.

In 1957 Bryant wasn't about to miss another chance. On November 9, Alabama's brand new and football-friendly president Frank Rose gathered a small group of board members and alumni to meet "secretly" with Bryant in Houston. (Word got out immediately, making Bryant's last weeks at A&M miserable. The newspapers reported his anticipated departure the day before his Aggies played against Rice. When his team lost, 7-6, and subsequently lost the national title, Bryant blamed the press.)

Bryant expressed several concerns in the meeting, including having to share duties with Hank Crisp, who also happened to be the man who recruited Bryant as a player! Crisp agreed to step aside so Bryant could serve as both head coach and athletic director. Bryant asked for and received a long-term (ten-year) contract. His salary was set at $17,500 a year. (At Bama, only the president made more than this!) In January he would move to Tuscaloosa. Help was on the way.

The dreadful 1957 season ended with a humiliating 40-0 loss to Bama's archrival, Auburn. A few days later, the front page of nearly every Alabama newspaper carried the news. Bryant was the new head coach.

In 1958, the year forty-four-year-old Bear Bryant came back to Alabama, I was a five-year-old kid living in Brooklyn, New York. I didn't know Bear Bryant from Smokey the Bear! So, I can't claim that I knew his hiring would be one of the most important milestones in the history of Alabama football. Even President Rose, who saw something special in Bryant, never claimed to have foretold that Coach Bryant's hiring would lead to glory days at Alabama beyond our wildest reckoning. No one knew that he would chalk up six national championships, thirteen SEC titles, and twenty-four consecutive bowl games as Alabama's coach. But no doubt about it, Alabama fans were excited. People thought at the very least, things were going to get better. As to becoming a winning program again? They couldn't help but hope.

The facts backed up the theory that Bryant was a winner. He had paid his dues, and his résumé spoke volumes. He had been an assistant coach in the SEC. He had a winning record his first year as a head coach at Maryland. He

Coach Bryant and his Aggie staff.

also had a winning record at the University of Kentucky. *Kentucky!* What were the chances of that? Coach Bryant had made it happen at a nontraditional football school.

Where Bryant really made his mark, though, was at Texas A&M. In his first year there he took his now legendary Junction Boys off campus over the summer and toughened them up boot-camp style. Imagine a coach today taking a team off-campus during a ninety-five-degree Texas summer, clearing a rocky dirt field, and setting them to doing intense two-a-days and at the end of the day having them crash in a non-air-conditioned dorm. The stories from this particular season defined Coach Bryant and preceded him as he prepared to return to Alabama.

This would be a good time to note that the Junction Boys stories were music to the ears of football fans but maybe not so sweet-sounding to the Alabama players waiting to meet their new coach. People had heard the stories, they knew Coach Bryant's name, and there was a lot of excitement surrounding his return to Tuscaloosa. Coach Clem Gryska, who joined Bryant's staff in 1960 and worked with him for twenty-four years, remembers the anticipation.

"Billboards went up around town welcoming him and Mary Harmon back," Gryska said. "People were excited."

Bryant moved his family to Alabama in January. Immediately, he got to work. There was a new sheriff in town. As happy as people were to have Coach Bryant back, it took a while for many folks to adjust to his style.

Author Tom Stoddard spends almost an entire chapter in his book *Turnaround*, describing one of Bryant's early meetings with his players during which he made his intentions clear. "I came here to make Alabama a winner again," he

The first family of Alabama football.

Photo courtesy of the Paul W. Bryant Museum, the University of Alabama.

said, adding gruffly that, "I don't know any of you and I don't want to know you. I'll know who I want to know after spring training."

He did manage to give the team some good news, telling them that things such as food, accommodations, modes of travel, and equipment were going to be first class. But then he let them know he expected first-class play and behavior in return.

"How many of you have written your mothers this week?" he demanded. "How many made up your beds this morning? How many of you went to church on Sunday? How many said your prayers last night?"

Of course, the main focus of the meeting was about winning.

"If you're not committed to winning ball games, to making your grades, go ahead and get your stuff and move out of the dorm, because it's going to show," Bryant said to a rapt group of players. "Pull out so we can concentrate on the players who want to play. You can have all the God-given ability in the world, but if you don't hustle, you won't play. We're going to start somebody else in your place."

Times had changed. The players knew it. But it wasn't just the players who had to adjust to the new coach. According to Clem Gryska, it took a while for local business boosters to accept Bryant's winning ways.

Working the phones.

Photo courtesy of the Paul W. Bryant Museum, the University of Alabama.

"There was a group of businessmen—bankers, doctors, real estate people—who used to meet at the hotel downtown and play gin and drink coffee. In years past, the head coach would join them there and the intimate ones, like the bank president, would come to the coach's office and sit around and visit. Well, right away Coach Bryant said, 'Off-premises is OK, gentlemen. But don't come to the office.' They were the richest boosters and he broke them off just like that. He said, 'I don't come to your office and drink coffee when you're writing a million-dollar loan.' When he was working, they weren't welcome."

Coach Bryant stopped the tradition of heading out for long lunches with the local business types. He also stopped the practice of letting them come to football practice.

"That made them mad," Gryska said. "He locked the gate. They couldn't get in and the players couldn't get out! If the players wanted to quit, they had to climb the fence. A couple of them did!"

Gryska says the boosters didn't stay mad long.

"It didn't take but three or four weeks until they understood what Bryant was doing," he said. "He was building the team. He felt like he was hired to win football games and that was what he intended to do."

For his part, Bryant tried to play down the high expectations and well-meaning excitement on the part of the

The man.

Photo courtesy of the Paul W. Bryant Museum, the University of Alabama.

fans and the media. At one of his early, preseason press conferences, a reporter said, "Coach, the alumni are expecting your team to go undefeated next season."

Bryant growled back at the guy: "The hell you say! I'm an alumnus, and I don't expect us to go undefeated."

He knew it might take a season or two to get rolling, especially since, as he put it, "I inherited a rag-tag bunch of players that I didn't recruit." But from the first day he stepped on the field for spring practice there was no mistaking the fact that he intended to turn the Crimson Tide into winners again. The hard work of getting there would begin on the practice field. Under Coach Bryant, practices were frequent, long, and administered with laser-beam focus.

"He was focused," Gryska said. "When someone got hurt, usually the trainer and the coach goes to them and everything would stop. But Coach Bryant would say, 'Move that drill!' And we'd keep on while the trainer was seeing to the hurt guy over there. Some people might say that was inhumane, but it got our attention. He'd say, 'Someone will see to that. It's not my job.'"

Coach Gene Stallings, who played and coached for Bryant at Texas A&M, came with him to coach at Alabama that year. Stallings said the coach had no choice but to get his team focused immediately.

"With some exceptions, the young men on the team were not as talented as the ones we had at A&M," Stallings said. "They were lacking in focus and had very little understanding of the sacrifices it was going to take to build a winning program."

Photo courtesy of the Paul W. Bryant Museum, the University of Alabama.

"Alright now . . . listen up!

They learned quickly. From the moment Coach Bryant erected his famous coach's tower, the players knew this was a new era. The seniors were the heroes of this group. Things were tough on them, especially since Bryant made it clear that he was rebuilding and they were a very low priority to him.

"I don't care if every senior in this room gets up and walks out," Coach Bryant said during one meeting with his veteran players. "Because for you to play, you're going to have to be twice as good as a junior or sophomore, and I doubt very seriously that any of you are."

Some twenty-two players quit the team in the spring, followed by sixteen more in the fall. The ones who stayed gained an enormous sense of pride as Bama set about playing the best football they had played in over a decade.

Working towards another win.

Photo courtesy of the Paul W. Bryant Museum, the University of Alabama.

Many people are nostalgic about the good ol' days of the 1950s. It's true, there's no comparison between the distractions today's college kids face versus those the players dealt with back then. Sure, they drank and ran around a little bit. But there was little drug use, if any at all. Agents weren't yet hovering around talented college kids like flies. There were no cable TV channels, DVDs, or cell phones. And NCAA rules were much more relaxed. Back then, a coach had many more scholarships at his disposal. No one worried about getting sued for not giving players enough water breaks. The times were simpler. But does that mean it was easy to accomplish what Coach Bryant did? Of course not. The next twenty-four years would prove that to be true.

I never worked with Bear Bryant, but I was in his presence a couple of times. All I got the chance to do was say hello and shake hands with the man, but I could see instantly that he was the kind of man who commanded respect. He was capable of walking through a door and completely captivating a room.

I have been really lucky during my career—I have had the opportunity to interview some of the biggest names in sports. I have interviewed Grambling State's Eddie Robinson, Penn State's Joe Paterno, and Muhammad Ali, among many others. I was impressed and very honored to spend time with these people. But I don't know if I was in awe of them. But when I saw how people dealt with Coach Bryant—even the seasoned, salty media guys—I have to say they treated him differently. They treated him with incredible reverence, and I found that very revealing.

He was an absolutely special and imposing person. People knew that from the moment he came home to Alabama in 1957. And the legend only got bigger and bigger over the years.

People were impressed by him from the moment he set foot in Tuscaloosa. As I said before, he had a history with the university. His first day back, he walked out onto Denny Field and said, "There's not a spot of ground out there that doesn't have a little bit of my blood on it."

Alabama fans hoped beyond hope that he was the guy they were looking for to pull the Crimson Tide out of the hole it had been in. And in a larger sense, Alabamians were looking for some redemption in the eyes of the rest of the country. There had been plenty of racial strife that had given the state of Alabama a black eye in this era. Football had always been a positive thing to point to. People in the state wanted those bragging rights back.

Did people know that bringing the Bear back to Bama was the key that was going to unlock zillions of memories? I don't know if anybody could honestly say that. But know it or not, when the whistle blew for the first spring practice in 1958, Bama was on track to a return to glory.

Technically, the Tide finished the 1958 season as winners (5-4-1). This certainly wasn't the best Bama would do, but what the numbers don't show is the fact that the groundwork had been laid.

The next couple of seasons showed the team getting progressively better. The 1959 season ended with Bama at 7-2-2. In 1960, they went 8-1-2. And then in 1961, just four short years after Bryant signed on as head coach, Bama would be crowned national champs.

Mama couldn't have been more proud.

The 1961 Championship

The Prophecy

IN 1961 IT BECAME OFFICIAL. BEAR BRYANT WAS A PROPHET.

When Bryant had returned to Alabama in 1958, he put his system in place, focusing on the youngest players he inherited on that team. In 1961 those young players had become seniors. The other players on the team, the juniors, sophomores, and a new crop of freshmen had all played for Coach Bryant from the start of their college football careers. In 1958 the Bear said, "We'll be national champions in four years." In 1961 it came true.

Tackle Billy Neighbors was a freshman when Bryant signed on as head coach in 1958.

"We were in the first meeting with Coach Bryant and he told us in four years, if we believed in his plan and dedicated ourselves to being the best we could be, we would be national champions," Neighbors said. "He was right."

Bryant's first year as head coach, 1958, was a turnaround year. Following a terrible blur of seasons under coach J. B. "Ears" Whitworth where Bama won only four games in three years, Coach Bryant's squad turned in a respectable 5-4-1 record.

The 1959 season was even better. The Tide finished 7-2-2 and, even more impressively, held their opponents to just fifty-nine points all season. Numbers like this reminded fans of the days when Coach Frank Thomas was at the helm. They couldn't have been happier. Bama tied Tennessee, 7-7, and beat Auburn, 10-0, that year, then capped off the best season in recent memory with a visit to a bowl game, a milestone considering the fact that Bama hadn't gone to a bowl in five years.

On December 19, 1959, Alabama met Penn State in the Liberty Bowl. (Interesting historical note: this was the first time Bama played against a black player, Penn State's Chuck Jenarette.) Unfortunately, the Nittany Lions put up the only score and won it, 7-0. But despite the loss, Bama was back in the proverbial "game." The "bowl game" in particular. Bama would play in bowls for the next twenty-five years in a row!

In 1960, things improved even more. Bama went 8-1-2, giving fans plenty of exciting games to cheer about along the way. Perhaps the most memorable game that season, especially in the eyes of the players, was the Georgia Tech matchup.

At halftime the Tide was down, 15-0. The players, well acquainted with their no-nonsense coach by now, expected a serious verbal lashing when they hit the locker room. Instead, Coach Bryant shocked his team by telling them,

The Coach at Birmingham's Legion Field.

Photo courtesy of the Paul W. Bryant Museum, the University of Alabama.

"Now we've got them right where we want them." The players looked at him dumbfounded as he continued, "Now they'll see what we've got in us."

Coach Bryant would use this brand of reverse psychology many times over the years. The quotes varied, "Now they'll see if we have any class," or "Let's show 'em what kind of team we really are," but the sentiment was the same and the coach employed it often over the years when his team was down. During this particular game, it worked.

The Bama defense held Georgia Tech scoreless in the second half while the offense went to work. Quarterback Pat Trammell threw a long touchdown pass in the fourth quarter to Leon Fuller. Then, when Trammell got hurt, backup quarterback Bobby Skelton, who later in life became an NFL official, finished the job, tossing to Norbie Ronsonet for another touchdown. Still trailing, the Tide came up with a field goal in the final seconds and won the game, 16-15.

The finale of the 1960 season was the Bluebonnet Bowl. The Tide played to a draw with the University of Texas, 3-3. Not exactly a thrilling conclusion but the best was yet to come. Enter 1961.

The banner says it all.

The veterans on the 1961 squad, the guys who had Coach Bryant as their coach from the start, make up a now legendary list of players that included Pat Trammell, Billy Neighbors, Lee Roy Jordan, Darwin Holt, Mike Fracchia, Butch Wilson, Billy Battle, Bill Oliver, and Tommy Brooker.

Regarding these legends in the making prior to the '61 season, a reporter asked Coach Bryant if he thought his team looked like a winner.

"You can't look at a rabbit and see how fast he can run," Bryant said.

No doubt about it, though, this rabbit was looking good. Billy Neighbors says Coach Bryant saw to it that when the season began, this team was in shape.

"He didn't like for you to be too big," Neighbors said. "He would give you a weight to have every year. If you didn't make that weight, he wouldn't give you a uniform. As a matter of fact, he kicked my brother off the team because he was two pounds overweight."

In December 1961, after the perfect 11-0 season, Coach Bryant revealed what he really had been thinking about his team before the first kickoff that year. "Regardless of who was coaching them, they still would have been a great team," he confessed. "I said early in the season that they were the nicest, even sissiest bunch I ever had. I think they read it, because later on they got unfriendly."

Hey, whatever works! Alabama not only won every game in 1961, they won every game by a lot. No one even came close. They held their opponents to twenty-five points all season. Again, shades of Frank Thomas—this was the fewest points allowed since the 1933 squad gave up just seventeen. Alabama outscored their opponents a stunning 297-25 in 1961.

Highlights of the season included the season opener against Georgia. Fullback Mike Fracchia scored the first touchdown of the year in the second quarter, and by game's end he had gained seventy yards in sixteen carries. The terrific Tide defense held the Bulldogs scoreless until the last play of the game. A few weeks later, Bama trounced North Carolina State, 26-7, in a game where Trammel outplayed rival quarterback Roman Gabriel to the tune of ten completed passes.

Perhaps most satisfying of all to Coach Bryant was when Bama got its revenge against Tennessee, taking the Vols down, 34-3. In *The Third Saturday of October*, the book about the Bama-Tennessee rivalry, Billy Neighbors tells a story about the aftermath of that game.

"Coach Bryant walked onto the team bus at the stadium after the game and told us we had a great team," Neighbors said.

"That was a big deal to us because he'd been telling us how lousy we were. Then he announced that he was gonna give us all a personal gift, a ring, because we'd beaten Tennessee. I've still got it, as do a lot of the other guys, a red stone with an 'A' inscribed in it. And as a lasting memento of the man who bought it and gave it to me, it has 'Paul Bryant' inscribed on it. It's one of my more prized possessions."

To the delight of fans and players alike, Bama secured big-time, statewide bragging rights in their final regular season game against Auburn, when they stomped the Tigers, 34-0. Auburn's coach Shug Jordan had this to say:

"I don't know if that's a great team, but they most certainly were great against us. I don't guess anybody has ever hit us that hard."

Pat Trammell, Lee Roy Jordan, and Billy Neighbors were named all-Americans and all-SEC in 1961. (For those keeping track, they were the first Alabama all-Americans since Ed Salem in 1950). Mike Fracchia also took all-SEC honors and was named Outstanding Player during the Sugar Bowl against Arkansas. (The Tide won, 10-3.)

What a year! Alabama won the national championship and the SEC championship. Coach Bryant won national-coach-of-the-year honors. Then, in anticipation of many more good years to come, the university expanded Denny Stadium (Note: it wouldn't be retitled Bryant-Denny until 1975), so that the next year it would seat up to forty-three thousand fans. Many of the fans that year were thrilled to watch the victories engineered by their tremendous quarterback, Pat Trammell.

One of the all-time Bama greats, Lee Roy Jordan.

Coach Bryant had his own, backhanded way of bragging on his star player: "He can't run. He can't pass, and he can't kick. All he can do is beat you."

He also said on more than one occasion: "As a quarterback, he had no ability. As a leader, I've never had another like him."

Charlie Pell, who was called "Little Charlie Pell" due to his relatively diminutive, 180-pound stature (for a tackle anyway), once gave a reporter an example of Trammel's leadership. "Pat Trammell was the top dog of that football team," Pell said. "I'll never forget; we had a big old tackle who would always want to call timeout. We were playing both ways then and everybody would want somebody else to call timeout. But if he couldn't get anybody else to say it, this tackle would. I remember Pat telling him to shut his damn mouth. Everybody knew he could back it up, too."

The late Pat Trammell—revered and respected to this day.

In his book, *100 Years of Alabama Football*, author Gene Schoor gives an example of how Trammell kept his freshmen rivals in line. According to Trammell's teammate, Bill Oliver, Trammell charged into a room where the younger players were sitting around a table, flipped a big switchblade knife into the tabletop, and, as the knife quivered back and forth, asked if any of them were quarterbacks. No one piped up.

"Right then," Oliver said, "they all became halfbacks."

While he didn't pull a weapon on Coach Bryant, Trammell was one of the few (if any) Alabama players to speak freely in his presence.

"He was probably the only guy that I knew that would talk back to Coach Bryant," Billy Neighbors said. "They'd send in a play and if Pat didn't want to run it, he wouldn't run it. He would just say, they don't know what the hell they are talking about. You would hear them fussing at each other coming down the sideline. Coach would be hollering at him; Pat would be talking back to him. He's the only one that I know of that got away with it. But most of the time, Pat was right. He was a great, great football player. We never lost a game when he started at Alabama. We lost three games, and Pat was hurt the three times we got beat."

Lee Roy Jordan agrees with Neighbors's assessment of Trammell. "He was a tremendous leader. Whatever he had to do, if it meant getting a first down or to keep the clock rolling or the chains moving or, you know, throw the ball out of bounds to keep from having a sack or get the ball in the end zone, running or passing. Whatever it took, he would do it."

Players who came after Trammell share his teammates' respect.

"What a tough guy he was," said Ken Stabler, who would step into Trammell's shoes just a few years later.

Wes Neighbors, who played center from 1983 to 1986 and who happens to be Billy Neighbors's son, has heard his share of stories about the old days. In particular he has heard how many players in his dad's era had to play both offense and defense. Wes was overheard giving the old man a hard time as he related the tale—evidently not for the first time—of having to be in amazing shape in 1961 in order to play fifty-eight minutes every game.

"I have to hear that story every day," Wes laughed. "It was like, 'Yeah, back then, we could fold up our helmet and put it in our back pocket!'"

All kidding aside, the younger Neighbors is perfectly willing to give credit where credit is due.

"I saw a film on Pat Trammell," he said. "I guess it was the '61 highlight film, where he actually pitches the ball on a sweep and makes a block fifty yards down field against Vanderbilt, the last block before they got the score. It wasn't just a block; it was a crushing block."

Bama never lost a game that Pat Trammell started.

Photo courtesy of the Paul W. Bryant Museum, the University of Alabama.

On the lighter side, assistant coach Dude Hennessey once told a story about how Coach Bryant sent another assistant to visit Trammell's parents in Scottsboro. One of the items on the agenda was to address Trammell's cussing; Coach Bryant had already established a system whereby players and staff would be fined every time they were caught saying curse words.

"So, he went by, and Mrs. Trammell came to the door," Hennessey said. "And she said, 'You old son of a buck'—I'm cleaning this up a little—'What in the hell are you doing up here?' He said, 'Well, I just come to visit with you.' She said, 'Well, you S.O.B. . . .' Then he went to see his daddy who says, 'Well, you ol' son of a buck, you haven't been up here in a long time. Get your butt back up here sometime.'"

The assistant returned to Tuscaloosa and, according to Hennessey, reported that Trammell was not likely to change his vocabulary anytime soon.

Jack Rutledge, Bryant's longtime assistant coach and a player on the '61 squad, saw the kind of unusual relationship Bryant had with Trammell:

"Coach Bryant would eat lunch with the quarterbacks," Rutledge said. "Then on game day, the team captains that were appointed that week would eat lunch with them, too. I was captain against Mississippi State that particular week.

"So the relationship we had with Coach Bryant, you know, you are not saying anything. You're sitting at the table eating and hoping the meal will get over with in a hurry. But Trammell is just sitting there eating like he normally does. Then Coach Bryant takes out a pen and drew a little thing on his napkin. He slides it in front of Trammell and says, 'Pat, what do you think about that play?' Pat keeps eating and says, 'I don't think that will work worth a damn.'"

It seems to be a unanimous opinion among former teammates and staff that Trammell was an amazing player who indeed spoke his mind to Coach Bryant and earned his respect. Coach Bryant favored Trammell. In fact, there is no question that he came to love him a great deal.

Sadly, in 1968, just seven years after he graduated from the University of Alabama, Pat Trammell died from a brain tumor.

"This is the saddest day of my life," Bryant said, when he heard the devastating news.

In remembering Trammell, Bryant said he was "probably the best" of all

Photo courtesy of the Paul W. Bryant Museum, the University of Alabama.

Coach Bryant said it best: "He couldn't pass and he couldn't run; all he could do was put points on the board and win games."

his quarterbacks, not bad company considering seven of the quarterbacks who played for him, including Joe Namath and Ken Stabler, went on to the pros. Interestingly, Trammell did not go on to the pros after college, but Bryant had every confidence he could have.

"Pat would have played in the NFL if he hadn't decided to be a doctor," Bear said. "He couldn't pass and he couldn't run; all he could do was put points on the board and win games. He called plays better than the coaches could, and he instinctively knew what the defense was trying to do. He was a tremendous leader. The players followed him around like they were following their mamas."

Unbeatable combination: Bear Bryant and Pat Trammell.

The 1961 season is a tremendous legacy for Trammell to have left behind. In a way, it marked the true beginning of the Bear Bryant era, in that it was the first national championship season of the six he would accumulate during his twenty-five-year career at Alabama.

If there was a negative aspect to this great year, it came when Bryant and his staff were criticized in the *Atlanta Journal* and later in the *Saturday Evening Post* for allegedly sanctioning brutality. The accusation came after Georgia Tech halfback Chick Graning sustained broken cheekbones, lost several teeth, and was knocked unconscious after a particularly tenacious block by Bama linebacker Darwin Holt.

The very next year, the *Post* came after Bryant again, this time accusing him of fixing the opening game of the 1962 season with University of Georgia then athletic director, Wally Butts. Bryant always vehemently denied these charges and ultimately won a $300,000 libel suit. Said Butts: "I don't know enough about the details of the situation to comment intelligently, but I will say it's beyond the scope of my imagination to believe Bryant would ever consider doing something that wasn't all about winning and by as many points as possible." Would the Bear we know do something like that for money? It's unfathomable.

In any case, the scandal turned out to be a small blip on a year that kicked off what would turn into a legendary run. The 1961 team would always be a hard act for future Bama teams to follow.

If it moved, Lee Roy could tackle it.

Barry Krauss, who played on Bama's 1978 championship team, heard Coach Bryant talk about this team many times, often referring specifically to Lee Roy Jordan's on-field gifts. "Coach Bryant always said, if they were standing between the sidelines," Krauss remembered. "Lee Roy will make the tackle."

If there had been any doubts prior to 1961 that Bryant intended to make his team a winner, they had all been washed away after this incredible season. The truly remarkable thing, though, was that it really was just a beginning. Some coaches could have retired happily after such a year. But at this point, Alabama fans hadn't even yet heard of players named Namath, Stabler, Musso, Lyons, Croom, Shula, or Bennett.

This was all still to come.

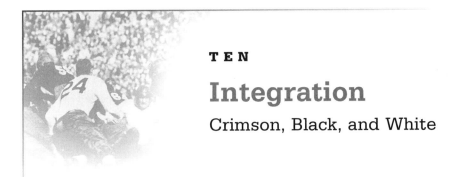

TEN

Integration
Crimson, Black, and White

ONE OF THE MOST SIGNIFICANT EVENTS IN THE HISTORY OF THE
football program at the University of Alabama occurred in the spring of 1970
when Wilbur Jackson became the first African-American player to be signed
to a football scholarship at the school. On the heels of this came the truly
historic moment in 1971 when John Mitchell became the first African-
American to actually play on the varsity team.

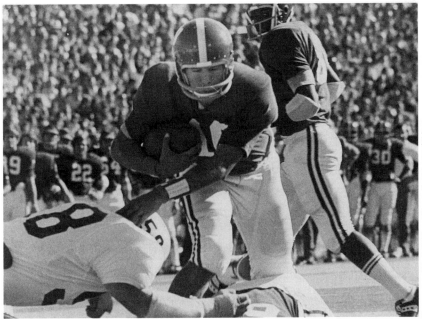

Ball-carrier Terry Davis, (#10) with Wilbur Jackson, (#80) in the background.

Photo courtesy of the Paul W. Bryant Museum, the University of Alabama.

As someone who wasn't living in Alabama at the time, it's difficult for me to speak in a knowledgeable way about what the atmosphere was like and how people felt about integration. But my impression is that under the leadership of Coach Bryant, who virtually could do no wrong as far as Alabamians were concerned, the transition to an integrated football squad, when it finally happened, was surprisingly smooth.

Coach Clem Gryska, Bryant's longtime assistant coach, says Bryant was interested in signing black players some twenty years before he actually did it.

A color-blind Bear.

"He tried to get black players when he was head coach at Kentucky," Gryska said. "But the school wouldn't let him. And he would have had black players here earlier, but he just had to wait for the right time."

I have never heard or read one word about Bryant being a bigot. It makes sense that a man who cared about fairness on the playing field ("I don't care who your daddy is") and being promoted on the basis of your ability would feel this way.

According to printed newspaper stories of the day, it was reported that the coach would visit black high school games around Alabama and worry that the terrific black players he saw would be going to other schools. And they did.

In 1959, a Bryant-coached team played against a black player, Penn State's Chuck Jenarette, for the first time when the Tide met the Nittany Lions in the Liberty Bowl. Jenarette and the rest of Penn State's terrific defense held Bama scoreless, and Penn State won it, 7-0.

Bama continued over the years to play against teams with black players. Then, in 1970, Bryant signed Wilbur Jackson, a tailback from Ozark,

Alabama, to a scholarship. That year, he was a freshman and couldn't play, but Jackson was on the team and his time was coming.

Newspaper reports indicate that representatives from the NAACP came to see Coach Bryant. He shocked them by inviting them into his office right away and agreeing with them that integration was long overdue. He proved it by opening his desk drawer and pulling out a list he had put together of the best black football players in the state.

He told the group that any of the players on this list would get a scholarship from him if they could be convinced to attend the University of Alabama. None of them did.

In 1970 Alabama hosted Southern Cal in the season opener at Birmingham's Legion Field. It was a game that is now pivotal in college football history. The Trojans absolutely embarrassed the Crimson Tide, crushing them, 42-21. To add salt to the wound, a black USC fullback, Sam "Bam" Cunningham, led the charge by scoring three touchdowns. Cunningham, who gained 135 yards on twelve carries, was spectacular.

Underscoring the message, another black player on the USC squad, halfback Clarence Davis, did his own share of running and scoring. Davis was born in Birmingham. Enough was enough.

Bryant was always all about winning. The fans were in full agreement. Bama already had Jackson, who would soon be ready to play. But Bryant was searching for another player to start immediately. Specifically, he wanted someone who would be ready for the rematch against Southern Cal in 1971. He found that man in John Mitchell, a Mobile, Alabama native, who had distinguished himself playing defensive end at Eastern Arizona Junior College.

Since Mitchell would be transferring from a junior college, he would be eligible to play right away. In fact, this was Bryant's main selling point when he first spoke to Mitchell and, later, his mother on the phone. When he learned Mitchell was open to the idea of playing for Bama, a recruiter was dispatched to Mobile to see him right away.

Mitchell remembers his now historic decision to have been a relatively easy one.

"I'd do it again in a minute," Mitchell said. "If you're a football player, you

Mobile's John Mitchell: the first African-American to play for Alabama.

Photo courtesy of the Paul W. Bryant Museum, the University of Alabama.

dream of playing for Coach Bryant."

Clem Gryska says Mitchell made a graceful transition to life on a mostly white campus and mostly white team.

"There were several black players that year, and I think the other players were very respectful of them because they were great athletes," Gryska said. "We had whites and blacks rooming together right away. John was just great. As soon as he came to spring practice, he played like gangbusters!"

Bryant paid Mitchell the ultimate compliment by giving him no preferential treatment. According to Clem Gryska, Bryant said many times, "When you get on the field, I don't care if you're red, white, blue, or purple. You better perform.'"

And perform, Mitchell did.

As Bryant had hoped, Mitchell broke out during his very first game, the season opener and grudge rematch against USC. Granted, this was the game where Bryant stunned USC by unveiling his new wishbone offense, which most people credit for Bama's victory. But Mitchell, playing linebacker, did his defensive part from the start by making a decisive tackle on the kickoff.

The Tide was on a roll that season—the team not only won all the rest of their regular-season games, they won by a landslide. Southern Miss? 42-6. Florida? 38-0. Ole Miss? 40-6. Vanderbilt? 42-0. In other words, they crushed every opponent, scoring a total of 362 points to the opponents' 84. They won the 1971 SEC championship and took a shot at the national title when they played Nebraska in the Orange Bowl. Sadly, "the big, ole cornfed boys" of

Nebraska, led by Johnny Rodgers, who broke Alabama's back with a seventy-seven-yard punt return prevailed, 38-6. Still, winning was again the flavor of the day at Tuscaloosa.

The 1972 season was a virtual carbon copy of '71. Then, during Bama's annual midseason test against Tennessee, it looked as though Bama might suffer its first loss of the season. The Tide was down, 10-3, with just minutes to go. Bama got the ball and three plays later, none other than halfback Wilbur Jackson ran two yards and dove in for a touchdown. Then, with just two minutes to go, Bryant stunned his players and fans by not going for a two-point conversion, which would have nailed the win. Instead, Bill Davis kicked the extra point to tie the game, 10-10.

John Mitchell explains what this meant to him. "Coach Bryant and (linebacker coach) Pat Dye showed a lot of confidence in the defense by not going for two and kicking the ball deep. So we knew the defense had to make a big play to win the game. We were hoping to force them into a mistake and get the ball back."

And that's just what happened. Bama defensive end Mike DuBose hit the Vols quarterback and knocked the ball loose. Mitchell recovered the ball at the Tennessee twenty-two. Bama quarterback Terry Davis ran it in for a touchdown on the very next play. Davis, DuBose, and, more significantly in a historical context—Mitchell and Jackson—were heroes. The Bama players, both black and white, broke out their victory cigars.

It was during halftime of this matchup in Knoxville (Bama was down, 3-0) where Mitchell first heard one of Coach Bryant's famous "come from behind" motivational speeches.

"He said we had them right where we wanted them," Mitchell said. "I remember wondering if he and I were watching the same game."

Another famous Bryant theme Mitchell would get to know that year: "He often told us that we didn't have to beat the other team," Mitchell said. "He said it was the other team's job to beat us because we were Alabama."

In 1972 John Mitchell led the team in sacks (he had twelve for a combined loss of eighty-one yards) and assisted tackles (seventy-five). Even more significantly, that year he became the first African-American at Alabama to earn all-American honors. He also was named cocaptain of the SEC championship team that year, another first for a black player. Wilbur

Mitchell became the first African-American assistant coach at the University of Alabama.

Photo courtesy of the Paul W. Bryant Museum, the University of Alabama.

Jackson, who played flanker his sophomore year and later switched to running back, was named co-captain of the team in 1973. After graduation in 1974, he became a first-round draft choice for the San Francisco 49ers, where he played for five years. He also played three years for the Washington Redskins.

While Jackson was busy entertaining visions of the NFL, Mitchell found himself marking another major milestone after graduation when he became the first African-American assistant coach at the University of Alabama.

Mitchell, who began his eleventh season as defensive line coach for the Pittsburgh Steelers in 2004, told a *Pittsburgh Post-Gazette* reporter about the day he got the Alabama job:

"I remember driving up to Tuscaloosa like it was yesterday," he said. "I'd graduated six months early, and I called Coach Bryant to see if there was something I could do for him while I was in graduate school. He said, 'I'm not gonna talk about it on the phone. Come up here and see me.' So I drove up from Mobile, about three and a half hours or so. I walked in and his secretary sent me in. He never even looked up. He said, 'I'm about to offer you a full-time job on my coaching staff. Are you going to take it?'

"I didn't know what to say," Mitchell continued. "But it was Coach Bryant. I said, 'Yes.' He said, 'Go to work.'

The Wizard of Oz: Ozzie Newsome.

Photo courtesy of the Paul W. Bryant Museum, the University of Alabama.

"I said, 'Coach Bryant, I don't have any clothes.' He looked at me and said, 'You'll be all right until Friday. You can go home then and get some.'"

Lesson: When you're about to make history, pack an overnight bag.

Mitchell was defensive line coach at Alabama for four years. He then spent the next six seasons as defensive line coach at Arkansas under Lou Holtz. After working for several other teams, including the USFL's Birmingham Stallions from 1983 to 1985, it was milestone time again when Mitchell became the first African-American defensive coordinator in SEC history when he accepted that position with LSU.

Mitchell is mostly upbeat about his experiences at Alabama. He told the *Post*, "Coach Bryant told me right in front of my mom and dad, 'You're probably going to have some problems coming here. I just want you to give me the first opportunity to solve those problems.' He said not to go to the press or anyone else, but you know, I never had to go to him."

Mitchell is still friends with his roommate from Alabama, Bobby Stanford, who happens to be white. He says he still calls Stanford's mom.

The strides Coach Bryant and the first African-American players made have left a wonderful, lasting legacy for generations of Alabama football

Ozzie caught them all.

The Tide without Derek Thomas, Cornelius Bennett and other African-American stars? Unthinkable.

fans to come. It's hard to imagine what Alabama football would have been like for the last thirty years without black players.

Dwight Stephenson: one of the best ever.

What if there had been no Ozzie Newsome? This incredible split end on the 1974-77 teams was named Alabama's Player of the Decade for the 1970s. Newsome, who started forty-seven consecutive games for Bama and caught 102 balls for 2,070 yards, helped his teams secure three SEC titles.

What if Quincy Jackson, Thomas Rayam, or Shaun Alexander had never been allowed to play at Alabama? What if we had never had Cornelius Bennett, another Player of the Decade for the 1980s, who also was a three-time all-American linebacker and SEC Player of the Year in 1986?

117

No David "Deuce" Palmer, no Freddie Milons, no Dwight Stephenson? Truly, it's unthinkable.

Looking to the future, maybe we all should take a page out of Coach Bryant's book. Here was a man who was definitely more interested in the color of a guy's jersey than in the color of his skin.

ELEVEN

Joe Namath

Joe Willie

TALK ABOUT A HOUSEHOLD NAME. EVERYBODY KNOWS JOE NAMATH. And before there were the Jets or pantyhose commercials, or Broadway Joe, Alabama had a guy they called Joe Willie.

When I was a kid growing up in Brooklyn in the sixties, my dad and I were season ticket holders for the New York Jets. Here came this guy—the word they used then was *mod*—here came this good-looking, mod guy who was an awesome quarterback. I loved him! We didn't care what he looked like or where he came from! He was a great player.

Touchdown Jets.

The big story then wasn't that he came from the University of Alabama. The big story was the unheard-of salary this guy would be paid, reportedly $427,000 for three years. This is still decent money today. Not for professional football players mind you, who might make that much in a game or two. But back then, four hundred grand was a lot of money. No one made that much. Not even close. This was an unprecedented figure. So, right away, when he came to New York, Joe Namath was famous.

This guy had the money, the looks, and now he had New York City at his disposal. He had the reputation of loving the nightlife and the ladies. He had this white llama rug in his apartment in the city. He dressed in big fur coats and bell bottoms.

But it wasn't all style for the guy who everybody began calling "Broadway Joe." When he came to New York, the owner of the new AFL team, Sonny Werblin, knew he had substance. He was a tremendous ballplayer. He was the superstar on whose shoulders this new franchise was going to be built.

Originally, New York's AFL team was called the Titans. They played at the decrepit old Polo Grounds, where baseball's Giants used to play and where the newly named New York Metropolitans (the Mets) would begin life.

Photo courtesy of the New York Jets.

Six more for Joe Wille.

Right before Namath came along, they tore down the Polo Grounds and put up the new ballpark, Shea Stadium, named after prominent lawyer Bill Shea. Since Shea was adjacent to the LaGuardia Airport runway, the team was named the Jets.

In New York, most football fans followed the Giants. They'd been around for years. The Jets were interlopers, They were the new people bringing in the ritz and the glitz. I don't think the term "nouveau riche" existed yet, but that's what they were. Then, very quickly, with a quality supporting cast and the great coaching of Weeb Ewbank, this team plunged right into uncharted territory. They began to win.

By January 1969, incredibly, the Jets were Super Bowl bound! This was so exciting. Even though we had season tickets, we couldn't afford to travel to the Super Bowl, which was played at the Orange Bowl in Miami, so my dad and I went over to our neighbors' house, the Spanglers, to watch. There weren't any big screen TVs yet, but their screen was bigger than ours. So that's where we went.

Of course the Jets were huge underdogs. Some writers had the Colts up by as much as twenty points. Then before the game, Joe made his famous claim regarding beating the Baltimore Colts. "We'll win," he said. "I guarantee it." Incredible.

I screamed and cheered during the whole game. Then, when they won and Joe trotted off the field holding up the "Number One" sign, it was magnificent. What a coming-out party. Every Jet fan earned immediate legitimacy on the shoulders of Joe Willie that day!

Joe was a huge star in the NFL. He was arguably the best-known athlete of his day, although a case could be made for Muhammad Ali as well. Certainly, he was the best-marketed athlete. Remember the shaving cream commercial he costarred in with an as-yet-unknown Farrah Fawcett? And the pantyhose spot? Only Joe Namath could put on pantyhose for a commercial without having his manhood questioned.

There is a great story about Namath that took place at a Jets dinner during his playing days. As people finished their dessert, speakers were coming up to the podium to give toasts. Jets linebacker Larry Grantham asked the audience to applaud the players' wives for all the sacrifices they'd made throughout the season. Namath then came up and said, "Let's give a hand to the single girls of New York who sacrificed just as much and complained a helluva lot less."

No doubt about it. The man was a superstar. But as odd as this sounds, he wasn't really cocky. Certainly not in an in-your-face way. He was confident. But during interviews he was always polite and respectful. Shy almost. Was it a function of his small-town upbringing in Beaver Falls, Pennsylvania? Or was it a function of his four years at the University of Alabama, where tradition and manners counted for something? Or was he thinking of what Coach Bryant might think?

Even when he was playing for a team that had won the Super Bowl, Joe Namath was often heard to say, "As Coach Bryant used to tell us . . ." He carried his experiences from Alabama with him. How could he not?

Joe Namath, the youngest of five children, grew up in Beaver Falls, Pennsylvania, a coal-mining town just outside of Pittsburgh. Young Joe excelled at football, basketball, and baseball in high school. In fact, he had an offer to play for the Baltimore Orioles but chose football. His first choice was Notre Dame. When that didn't work out, he thought about Maryland, but he

Namath lights up the scoreboard.

Photo courtesy of the Paul W. Bryant Museum, the University of Alabama.

didn't get in after coming up short on the college boards. It was then that assistant coach Howard Schnellenberger alerted Coach Bryant to Namath's availability. "Coach suggested I go on up to Beaver Falls and get Joe to Alabama."

So, in the fall of the very exciting national-championship year of 1961, Joe Namath showed up in Tuscaloosa. In Gene Schoor's book, *100 Years of Alabama Football*, Namath recalled his first day in town:

> Somebody took me out to football practice and Coach Bryant was up on the observation tower, watching and yelling and frowning on nearly every play. He waved his arms at me, so I climbed up on the tower to him. He introduced himself, I introduced myself. And honest, I didn't know what the hell he was talking about.

Photo courtesy of the *Birmingham News*

Mutual respect and admiration.

Former players have made a note of this historical moment. Not for the unmemorable (from Joe's point of view) exchange but for the fact that no players ever got invited up onto the coach's big, sturdy iron tower. At any rate, it wouldn't be long before Coach Bryant would make himself understood to the young Pennsylvanian.

"The freshmen were scrimmaging one night, and I ran out to my left on an option play, and as I started to pitch out, some big lineman hit me and the ball fell loose," Namath said. "I didn't scramble for the ball. Hell, the guy who made the tackle was holding on to me for dear life. It seemed he didn't want to get up either. Coach Bryant came out and said, 'Goldarn it, Namath, it's not your job to pitch the ball out and lay down there on the ground and not do anything.' He kept grumbling and I started to walk away toward the huddle, half listening to him and not looking at him. Suddenly, he grabbed hold of my face mask and yanked it around, nearly lifting me off my feet.

"'Namath!' he shouted, "When I'm talking to you, boy, you say, 'Yes sir,' and look me in the eye. I don't like no sideways looks.' He scared me half to death. From that day on, if Coach Bryant just said, 'Joe', even if I was fifty or sixty yards away, I'd run like hell to him, stop a yard away, come to attention, and say, 'Yes sir, Coach.'"

On a lighter note, Coach Bryant usually said more than just "Joe." He took to calling Namath, "Joe Willie," in the double-named, southern style of the Billy Bobs and Danny Joes of the region. It was a funny, affectionate nickname that stuck. Between bouts of tough love, of course.

During Namath's first season as a starting quarterback, he was struggling during the Vanderbilt game, and Coach Bryant yanked him from the field.

"I was really mad as hell," Namath said. "I threw my helmet down on the ground as I came off the field. I came over to the bench and sat down and Coach Bryant came over, sat down next to me, and put his arms around me."

Fans looking on may have thought the Coach was comforting his young star. But Namath later set them straight. "He was damn near squeezing my head off," he said. "'Boy,' he said, 'Don't let me ever see you come out of a game throwing your helmet around and acting like a show-off. Don't ever do that again.'"

Joe Namath is armed and dangerous.

Photo courtesy of the Paul W. Bryant Museum, the University of Alabama.

Namath explained he wasn't mad at the coach. Just at himself for playing so poorly. Somehow that season, coach and quarterback managed to meet in the middle. Bama went on to win all its games in 1962 except for one. (Georgia Tech squeaked by them, 7-6.) Unfortunately, this loss kept them from the SEC and national title that year, but the Tide wrapped the season in a bow at year's end when it crushed Oklahoma, 17-0, in the Orange Bowl. (Note: President John F. Kennedy performed the coin toss!)

The 1962 season was a welcome relief to Bama fans who feared the team might falter after losing the star seniors of 1961. But Namath was surrounded by great players, including four who went on to become head coaches: Bill Battle, Richard Williamson, Charlie Pell, and Jimmy Sharpe. Even though Coach Bryant was never a fan of the passing game, he couldn't deny that Namath had an amazing arm. Fans hadn't seen exciting passing like this since Harry Gilmer's day!

In 1963 Bryant switched to a pro-style offense, so as to better utilize Namath's many talents. Bama lost only two games, to Florida and Auburn. The season was rolling along when—with just two games left in the regular season—Coach Bryant was faced with one of the toughest decisions of his career. Word got back to Bryant that Namath had been out drinking and carousing off campus—a clear violation of team rules. This infraction seems like something straight out of *Leave it to Beaver* compared with stuff that goes on with players of today. But Bryant built his team's success by doling out discipline to stars and reserves alike. Bama fans will find it interesting to note that he polled his coaches regarding this situation. All but one voted to discipline but not suspend Namath. The dissenter? Future Bama head coach Gene Stallings.

"It was straightforward to me," Stallings said. "I felt like he had violated a rule. Joe was a great player and a great person. I thought in order for Coach Bryant to get the most out of Joe the following year, he had to get his attention."

BRYANT CALLED NAMATH INTO HIS OFFICE AND TOLD HIM WHAT HE had heard. Joe admitted that yes, it was true. Bryant gave kudos to Namath for telling the truth. But he was kicked off the team nonetheless.

Namath asked him how long the suspension would be. "For the year," Bryant answered. "Or forever. Or until you've proved something to me."

To the dismay of Bama fans, it was announced the Crimson Tide would play its last two games, a regular season matchup against Miami and the Sugar Bowl against Ole Miss, without Joe Namath. No. 2 quarterback Jack Hurlbut took over for the Miami game, and No. 3 guy, Steve Sloan, came in against Ole Miss. Bama won both games and Namath won Coach Bryant's admiration by not quitting the team. He could have transferred just about anywhere or accepted an offer to play in the Canadian Football League. But Namath stuck it out.

Years later, Namath told a journalist, "I deserved that suspension 100 percent. No, make it 110 percent."

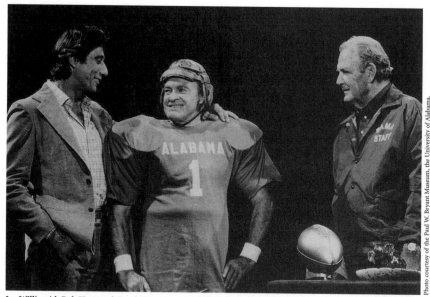

Joe Willie with Bob Hope and Coach Bryant on one of Hope's popular TV specials.

Photo courtesy of the Paul W. Bryant Museum, the University of Alabama.

In 1964 Namath was back after convincing his coach that he had mended his ways. After a perfect 10-0 season, Bama won the national championship that year. Everybody was happy.

There was one small cloud on this terrific season for Namath, who by this time was well known to be well on his way to a promising NFL career. During the Tide's fourth game of the season against North Carolina State, Namath, who had already completed seven of eight passes, cut across the field on a running play. He slipped on the grass and lay on the field hurt. He limped off the field and wrapped up his knee. Later, doctors told him he had sustained a double-cartilage tear. Sadly, this injury would plague him the rest of his life.

It's amazing that he became arguably the best quarterback in the NFL despite the bad knee. Until this 1964 injury, Namath had utilized running almost as much as passing in his game. He now had to alter that. In the NFL, his body took even more of a pounding. A comparison can be made with other legendary athletes who played hurt—Mickey Mantle comes to mind. What would he have been like without injuries? The thought is staggering.

Namath shared quarterback duties with Steve Sloan through the remainder of the highly successful 1964 season. The grand finale of the season and Namath's college career was the Orange Bowl against Texas. Bama ended up with a controversial loss, when, in the last seconds of the game, Namath appeared to run it in for the score. One referee said, "Touchdown." The other said, "No score." After talking it over, the officials ruled that Tommy Nobis and the Texas line had stopped Namath and called the game for the Longhorns.

Coach Bryant still had one more lesson for Joe Namath, who despite being named MVP of the game, was disappointed with the loss. He slumped on the bench, took a drink of water, threw the cup on the ground, and said, "I know I scored!" Coach Bryant fired back, "Get inside the dressing room. It didn't make any difference. If you can't jam it in from there without leaving any doubt, you don't deserve to win."

Namath quickly shook off the loss. As everyone knows now, before the Orange Bowl game of 1964, he and Coach Bryant had met with Sonny Werblin, the owner of the Jets. Namath made a verbal agreement to later sign a contract that would make him the highest-paid player in pro football history. Of course, all contact with the Jets was done properly under the rules of the day.

Werblin later told a reporter, "I offered him a Coca-Cola and he refused. He said Coach Bryant told him he was not to accept a damned thing until that game had been played."

Interestingly enough, a few weeks after that pre-Orange Bowl meeting, Coach Bryant himself accepted a very pivotal gift. Bryant's longtime assistant coach Clem Gryska tells the tale:

Werblin was so appreciative of getting Joe that he sent the coach a couple of hats. Coach Bryant used to wear Fedoras, the elegant ones with the rim and the feather on them. But Sonny sent him one of these houndstooth hats and he liked it. So, Sonny sent him a red one, a blue one, and a green one!

So Joe headed North, keeping his adopted, slight Alabama drawl as a keepsake. (He still has it.) He went on to become a pop culture icon, not to mention one of the most exciting players to ever play pro football.

Namath was inducted into the Pro Football Hall of Fame in 1985. His accomplishments are so numerous, it's hard to know where to begin. He won the AFL Rookie of the Year (1965), and the George Halas and Pro Player of the Year Awards (1969). He was the first pro quarterback to pass for more than four thousand yards in a season (1967). He led the league in passing yards and TDs thrown and was named to the Pro Bowl (1972). Oh yeah, and there's that Super Bowl ring.

Photo courtesy of Kent Gidley, the University of Alabama.

Alumnus Joe Namath delivers the football to mid-field to start a Bama home game.

What I find most intriguing though, is the story of Joe Namath. He has had some very public problems with alcohol in the last few years, which he has addressed openly. I respect that. I also respect the fact that he never forgets where he came from. In his Hall of Fame acceptance speech, his eyes welled with tears as he said, "Coach Bryant, Mrs. Bryant, wherever you are, we miss you."

When he comes back to visit the Alabama campus, which is often, Joe Willie carries instant credibility—not to mention huge celebrity—with him. He will come to Tuscaloosa from time to time and talk to the players at practice. He's always welcome there, and he is most certainly always welcome in our broadcast booth. Indeed, he has gone on the air with us many times. The minute he walks through the door I'm like a kid in a candy store. When he sits down next to my color man Ken Stabler, I am smart enough to know it's just my job to call the play and then shut up. I just let them go.

Joe Willie Namath. What a player. What a story!

TWELVE

Ken Stabler

The Snake

SINCE 1998 MY PARTNER IN THE BROADCASTING BOOTH, MY COLOR man, has been none other than Kenny "The Snake" Stabler. This beloved Alabama star quarterback who later went on to an incredible NFL career, where among many other things he led the Oakland Raiders to victory in Super Bowl XI in 1977, is a natural, gifted broadcaster. Obviously, he has "been there—done that" credibility that I could never hope to have. I've never taken a snap! He knows what he's talking about. So it's great having him sitting next to me on game day.

People often ask me, "What does Kenny do for a living?" My answer is, "He's Ken Stabler for a living." I'm not being a wise guy here. I'm being sincere. Like many retired superstar athletes, he makes speeches for different groups or plays golf at corporate outings. His job is being Ken Stabler. And he is great at it.

Photo courtesy of Kent Gidley, the University of Alabama.

The Snake.

Traveling with the Snake is like being on the road with a rock star. Many times I've had grown men pull me aside and say, 'Is that Ken Stabler?' Then they turn to putty. He is a genuinely nice person— I've never seen him turn down a request for an autograph, and people ask him every day. When he comes to the campus in Tuscaloosa to broadcast our pregame show on the quad, a long line forms instantly. Snake smiles and patiently, happily greets each person, slapping them on the back and posing for photos. I'm always amazed at the stuff people will schlep with them—old Raiders helmets, pictures from the sixties—in hopes of getting it signed by him. Kenny always obliges.

Kenny is a real Alabama boy, born and raised in the town of Foley, just outside of Mobile. He excelled in all the sports he played, especially football—he was an all-state quarterback in high school and pretty much had the pick of where he would go to college. Then he met Bear Bryant.

"That was it!" Kenny laughed. "He was so big and had that face that looked like it should have been carved in Mount Rushmore. Coach Bryant was the most imposing figure I had ever seen, next to my father. He looked just like him! They could have been brothers!"

By 1964 everyone in Alabama knew who Bear Bryant was. And every high school football player wanted to play for him. If he came to visit you in person, and charmed your mom and dad, it was pretty much a done deal. They would all but give their kid to him.

"When Coach Bryant came down to Foley and had dinner with my family, he didn't make any sales pitch to me," Stabler said. "He just talked about hunting and fishing and hypnotized us with his great voice."

Who is this young guy?

Kenny thought briefly about playing baseball in college, but after Bryant came to call, that was it. Plus, as I've heard him say, he thought you could make more money playing football! So, with just a few bucks to his name, he came to Tuscaloosa. A coach arranged for him to get a job mowing lawns to make some money.

Kenny came to the University of Alabama as a freshman in 1964. Joe Namath was a senior and the star quarterback of the national championship team. As Yogi Berra used to say, it was déjà vu all over again. When Namath came to Bama as a freshman in 1961, he stood on the sidelines and watched

Mickey Mantle has the Bama contingent's total attention.

senior Pat Trammell lead the team to the national title. Now, in his first year, the left-handed Stabler stood by and watched Namath and company do their thing. Maybe it's all about having really big shoes to fill.

It was another golden national championship year in 1965 (Bama went 9-1-1). Steve Sloan was the starting quarterback. But Kenny did well in practice and was thrilled when he was given the No. 12 jersey—the same one that Trammell and Namath had worn. Again, big shoes to fill.

Kenny, who by now was referred to as "Snake" by his teammates due to his elusive, swerving running style, did see some playing time in 1965, both at defensive back and at quarterback. Unfortunately, one

A rough day at the office. (But he won).

of his turns at quarterback produced one of Bama's most infamous results.

The Crimson Tide was playing Tennessee at Legion Field. The score was tied, 7-7, late in the fourth quarter. The clock is ticking. After a terrific series of passes that got Bama downfield, on third down the Snake scrambled for fourteen yards to the four-yard-line. Still, the clock is running. The kicker is ready to come in, but Snake lined up the offense and called "99 Quick." Then, in a moment he'll never forget, he threw the ball out of bounds to stop the clock. He thought it was first down. But it was fourth. Tennessee got the ball back and the game ended in a tie.

Coach Bryant loathed ties. He famously said, "A tie is like kissing your sister." So, after this particular incestuous kiss, another legendary moment in Alabama football history occurred when a furious Bryant proceeded to kick down the locked locker room door.

Bama tackle Jerry Duncan was there: "He literally knocked the door down. I mean right off its hinges. A policeman came in and asked who knocked the door down, and Coach Bryant said, 'I did.' The policeman just said, 'OK' and walked off."

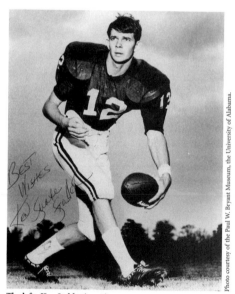

The lefty Ken Stabler in action.

Live and learn. In 1966 the Snake made few, if any mistakes. He also had a little offensive help from his friends, including receivers Ray Perkins and Dennis Homan. Bama went 11-0 and won the SEC title that year. Even though the national title technically eluded them (they finished third), it was a matter of timing. Both the UPI and the AP decided to name their number one picks before the bowl games. So, since Bama was technically No. 3 at the end of the regular season, that's where they stayed. Most people thought Alabama deserved the national crown, especially after their stunning 34-7 Sugar Bowl victory over Nebraska.

Photo courtesy of the Paul W. Bryant Museum, the University of Alabama.

Snake's 1967 Run in the Mud against Auburn.

The Sugar Bowl was a one-sided affair, to say the least. On the very first play, Stabler hit Perkins with a forty-five-yard pass. It went on in glorious fashion from there. Snake was named MVP of the game and still had another Alabama season, his senior year, to look forward to.

Then in 1967, during a run-of-the-mill drill at spring practice, the Snake tore cartilage in his knee. Coach Bryant told him to stay off it and not to practice until it was healed.

You know what they say about idle hands. Or in this case, idle knees.

"I got kind of bored because I couldn't practice," Snake said. "So, I started going to visit my girlfriend down in Mobile. We had study hall from 7:30 to 9:00. I would skip study hall, jump in the car and drive four hours to Prichard, Alabama, hang out with this girl I was seeing down there for four hours, jump back in the car and drive four hours back to try to make a 7:00 class. But I didn't make many of those."

"Well, one thing led to another. I kept going back and forth down there, not going to school. Then one day, I got a telegram at my parents' house. It said, 'You have been indefinitely suspended.—Coach Paul W. Bryant.' Then,

I got another telegram the very next day from Namath. It said: 'He means it.'"

So, Snake sucked it up and enrolled in summer school. He had to take and pass a lot of tough classes to get his eligibility back. But nothing was tougher than making the long trek into the coach's office.

"It was the hardest thing I've ever had to do!" Snake said. "I was so intimidated by that toughness and fairness about him. You go in his office and that desk is raised and that couch is soft and you sit way down under his eye level. So, I go in there and say, 'Coach, I have done everything necessary to become eligible by SEC standards; my grade point is back up and I want to come back out for the team.'

"He spits his tobacco, then looks me dead in the eye and says, 'You don't deserve to be on this team; get your ass out of here.'

"I said, well, I am going to come back out anyway, Coach." He said, 'We'll see.'

"So, I went out for practice and (coaches) Jimmy Sharpe and Pat Dye took great care of me, keeping me going straight. They came back to me and said, 'Coach Bryant says you can come back out for the team.'"

Kenny was thrilled. In his mind at least he had worked his way back and would pick up where he left off after the glorious success of last season. But he was getting a little ahead of himself.

"I was excited and got back out there for the first day of practice in the fall," Kenny said. "In practice, your uniform color dictates the team you're on. Red jersey, first team. White jersey, second team. Blue jersey, third team. Orange jersey, fourth team. Green jersey, fifth team.

"Well, Coach Bryant had this thing he would call you when you were out of favor with him—a turd. Been called that a hundred times. So here I was, after being MVP in the Sugar Bowl the year before and when I get my basket, it had a brown jersey in it. He made me work myself back to the top!"

No question. Coach Bryant was consistent.

"He taught me that no one player is any more important or bigger than the team itself," Snake said, "He treated everybody the same, from the groundskeeper to the bus driver to the president of the school. To him, we were all in it together. We are all the same."

Years later, we know that Kenny's jersey went from brown to crimson that fall. But Snake didn't know it until the last possible minute.

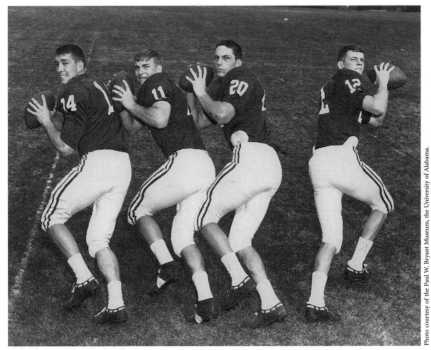

Photo courtesy of the Paul W. Bryant Museum, the University of Alabama.

Snake always goes his own way.

"We were playing Florida State in the opener," Stabler said. "Joe Kelley started the game. We went three and out. On the second series, we got the ball. I was standing there beside Coach Bryant, waiting to go in. Then, he hit me in the back so hard it knocked the breath out of me. He said, 'Go ahead!'"

But Coach Bryant's lessons for Stabler and his teammates were by no means over for the year. They were just beginning. Bama tied Florida State, 37-37, that day, and we all know how Coach Bryant felt about ties.

"He took us back to Tuscaloosa and we were out there at 6:00 A.M. the next morning," Stabler remembered. "We were out there doing that goal-line thing. Over and over."

The rest of the season was a good one, Bama finished 8-2-1. If the year was slightly marred by a loss to Tennessee, then at least it ended on a positive note when Bama rounded out the regular season with a thrilling 7-3 win over Auburn on December 2. And that game, arguably the most memorable of his college career, was all about Kenny Stabler.

"I played fifteen years of pro football and that's the worst weather I've

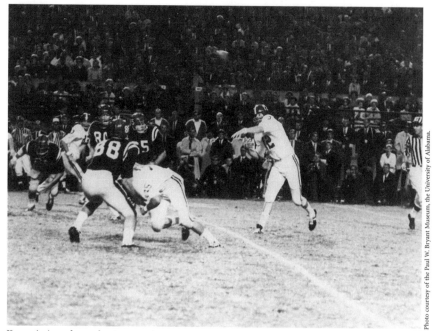

Kenny airs it out for another Bama touchdown.

ever played in!" Stabler said. "The field was six inches deep in mud and water. And it was real, real windy. If you look at old pictures, the fans' umbrellas are all turned inside out! So, before the game, Coach Bryant says we are not going to throw the ball. We are going to run the ball and control the line of scrimmage. When Auburn screws up its kicking game, we will play for field position and try to do something."

The game remained scoreless as the fans sat on the edges of their sopping wet seats. Then, in the third quarter, Auburn put three points on the board, courtesy of a John Riley field goal. But Bama caught a break in the fourth quarter when Auburn's punter mishandled a snap, and the Tide took the ball at their forty-six yard line. They made two short plays, gaining about seven yards. Then came the option play. Stabler saw a hole and just sloshed right through it. Bama wins 7-3.

"Once I started running, I just went straight for that chain-link fence!" Stabler said. "It was just a simple option. It happened just like Coach Bryant said it would. They screwed up the kicking game and gave us our opportunity."

Most likely, it was more than a good game plan that got it done for Bama that day. Stabler has many times talked about Coach Bryant's ability to motivate his players.

"He was intimidating," Stabler said. "I mean, I just stared at him all the time. But it was more than that. There was something about him that made you want to please him. You would do anything you could to have him slap you on the ass and say, 'Way to go,' and recognize you in front of the rest of the team."

Many former players concur. They also say he made you believe.

The Coach told Snake, "Throw it long."

Photo courtesy of the Paul W. Bryant Museum, the University of Alabama.

"I remember playing in the '66 Sugar Bowl against Nebraska," Stabler said. "They were a heavy favorite. They were a much bigger, stronger team than we were. It had been drizzling all weekend long in New Orleans and a wet field probably favored Nebraska, a team that ran the ball a little better than we did. So, we're coming out of the locker room. It had been drizzling all weekend but I swear to God, when Coach Bryant stepped on the field it quit raining! It did!

"So, we're walking down the sideline to midfield getting ready for the first play of the game and he was smoking one of his unfiltered Chesterfields and looking out from under that houndstooth hat. He says, 'Stabler, I want you to throw the ball— throw the son of a bitch just as far as you can on the very first play.'"

So, Perkins does this little down and out and catches it. We scored six or seven plays later. For all practical purposes, the game was probably over."

Snake credits the coach.

"It was just the way he said things and phrased things," Stabler said. "We would always play teams that were bigger and faster, but we always won. I think he outcoached and outmotivated the other guy. We only lost three games in three years, and that was because of how great a coach he was."

Coach Bryant's record speaks for itself. Without question, he had a major effect on Snake and so many other players. They carried Coach Bryant with them their entire lives.

"I'm not your basic conformist," Snake laughed. "Coach Bryant was tough on me for my own good. I'd be bartending or selling cars or God knows what if it wasn't for him. I needed guidance."

Again, not to take away from the Coach but Snake deserves some credit here. Lightning did strike twice for him. He went on to carve out a one-of-a-kind NFL career.

In 1968 he was drafted by the Oakland Raiders. He played his first few years as third-string quarterback behind Daryle Lamonica and George Blanda. Snake went on to distinguish himself as part of this unforgettable, renegade Raiders team, led by Coach John Madden. Stabler took over as starting QB in 1973. The Raiders made it to the AFC championship game five consecutive times. In 1977 the Snake-led Raiders won Super Bowl XI.

Stabler, who still holds the Raiders team records for passing attempts, completions, yardage, and touchdowns, was a Raiders fan favorite because he was so exciting to watch. Still the Snake, he was terrific at switching directions and improvising on the run. He played for the Raiders until 1979, when he was traded to the Houston Oilers. Again, the shadow of Bear Bryant loomed large: his coach there was Bum Phillips, who had worked with Bryant at Texas A&M.

When Stabler was on his way to Houston, Phillips conferred with Coach Bryant.

"I didn't exactly go into that trade blind," Phillips told a reporter. "I knew a little about Kenny. I called Coach Bryant. He said, 'Don't believe all you've heard. He's a great kid. He'll do whatever you ask of him. He's a winner."

Snake won a Super Bowl quarterbacking the Oakland Raiders.

Photo courtesy of Ken Stabler.

Stabler finished his career in New Orleans, retiring at age thirty-six. He retired from football, that is. He can never retire from his other job—being Kenny Stabler.

He is one of the most at-ease people I've ever known. Whether he's at home on One Island, Alabama, or visiting in Tuscaloosa, he loves to go out, have a good time, and rub elbows with the fans. He never seems to grow tired of it.

Every year Kenny is on the list to be voted into the Pro Football Hall of Fame. Regretfully, he hasn't made it yet, which I think is a travesty. I have no argument at all with those who are in the Hall. But tell me, how is this guy left out? He was at the forefront of the Raiders' glory years. He was a Superbowl champion, a five-time pro-bowler, twice all-pro, three times all-AFC, and twice AFC Player of the Year. He notched thirty-six 200-yard passing games and at one point had 143 pass attempts without an interception (a Raider record). He also led the NFL in passing touchdowns in 1974 and 1976. I think this is Hall of Fame stuff. Regardless, Hall of Fame or not, no one can take away the fact that when he played, he won. That's what we remember.

So, on Saturdays in the fall, we sit in the broadcast booth and talk football. What could be better?

There's only one "Snake."

THIRTEEN

The Wishbone

Keeping Your Options Open

WHEN WE THINK OF BEAR BRYANT, WE THINK OF A GUY WHO IS decisive. Unshakeable. We think of a tough man who sticks to his guns.

But here's a surprise. This most unflappable, unmovable of mountains achieved some of his greatest successes by being adaptable. The best example of this was the introduction of the famous wishbone offense in the early seventies.

After the 1969 and 1970 seasons, Coach Bryant knew things had to change. Bama had been on a downslide. Since 1958, when Bryant first came to Alabama as head coach, Bama had chalked up ten winning seasons, complete with three national championships and four SEC titles. Then, in '69 and '70, things started to slip. The Tide went just 6-5 both years. (adding one tie to 1970s tally.) Especially painful were the losses to Auburn and Tennessee both years.

Making a "wish" bone.

When Bama tied Oklahoma in the New Year's Eve 1970 Bluebonnet Bowl, that was the last straw for Coach Bryant. The minute he boarded the plane back to Alabama from Houston, he had his pencils and paper out, working on a plan. Earlier, he had hinted to a reporter what he might be thinking about when he said, "Oklahoma ran up and down the field on us. Looks like Alabama didn't know much about stopping the wishbone."

The wishbone offense was indeed difficult to stop. Coach Bryant wondered, *Was it time to try something new?*

All-American John Hannah

Photo courtesy of the Paul W. Bryant Museum, the University of Alabama.

"In the late sixties, we had been throwing the ball a lot," said Coach Clem Gryska. "The passing team did a lot of laterals and finesse stuff, and that wasn't Coach Bryant. He was more like, 'If you're gonna try to block me, I'm gonna try to block you.'"

Indeed, it was well known that Bryant was not a huge fan of the pass. He often said, "There are only three things that can happen when you pass and two of them are bad."

He was also known to be a huge believer in defense, stopping just shy of saying a good "D" was all you needed to win games. But as anyone who can do a little math knows, it takes more.

All-American offensive guard John Hannah, basically the anchor of the team in '71, saw this firsthand.

"Offense has got to score points," Hannah said. "Defense will get you there, but offense has got to win it."

So, the very defense oriented, pass-wary Coach Bryant decided to make a change. According to *The Legend of Bear Bryant* author Mickey Herskowitz, after spring practice that year, Bryant went to visit his friend Coach Darrell Royal at the University of Texas, who had been perfecting a new system which was becoming popular in places like Texas and Oklahoma.

"He called about the wishbone and asked if I would spend time with him," Royal said. "I said, 'Yeah, I'd be glad to,' and he said, 'No, I mean real

Wishbone student and mentor Bear Bryant and Darrell Royal met in the 1973 Cotton Bowl.

time. Can we get a projector, go somewhere, and not have any phone calls or interruptions?'"

According to Herskowitz, Bryant actually moved in with the Royals, who were living in an apartment near the Texas campus while their home was being remodeled. As Bryant suggested, they set up a projector and went to work. But it didn't take long. After just one morning looking at film, Coach Bryant said, "Well, you can shut that damned thing down. I've seen all I need. I've decided to go with the wishbone."

Coach Bryant then asked Royal another enormous favor. He wanted to know if he could call him anytime, promising to keep his phone calls short and to the point. Royal agreed that Bryant could call him anytime he wasn't on the field. Indeed, Bryant and Royal maintained a virtual hotline to each other that year.

It's funny, as anyone who has visited the Bryant Museum in Tuscaloosa knows, Coach Bryant kept a bright red phone on his desk, which is on display there. People often joke that it was a direct line to the White House, but folks at the museum confirm it was merely a gift from the phone company, for which Bryant did commercials. But now that I think about it, was it his hotline to Royal? I digress.

The hotline?

There was a tight connection between the two coaches that year. Bryant welcomed Royal and his offensive coaches to Tuscaloosa in the spring for a clinic. And later that fall, the two schools swapped game films every week.

Just before the start of fall practice in '71, Bryant decided it was time to let his players in on his plans. "We're going to sink or swim with the Texas stuff," he said. "This isn't a trial, it's a commitment."

The wishbone was obviously a vast departure for Alabama. Other than the center snapping the ball to the quarterback, there's very little resemblance to any other offense. But at this point, the players, plus the Alabama and Texas coaching staffs, were the only ones privy to the coach's plan. Incredibly, the fact that Alabama planned to run the wishbone that year was to be kept a secret until they sprang it into action during their first game.

During the opening game of the previous season, Bama was beaten badly in Birmingham by Southern Cal. This year, they were determined to avenge the drubbing.

"They had beaten us 46-21 the year before, so we went out there with the wishbone offense and beat them," Hannah said. "We beat the same team with a whole new offense we'd learned in just three weeks. The most satisfying picture I have ever seen, still to this day, is a picture at that line of scrimmage. Our offensive line is coming off the ball low. We have already taken our first step and Southern Cal's defensive line hasn't even lifted their hands off the ground yet. To me, that was the most satisfying victory of my career."

As Hannah pointed out, the Bama players had just three weeks to learn the new offense. The lessons began under a literal shroud of absolute secrecy— a tarp was hung around the practice field fence to discourage onlookers. In fact, most of the practices were closed to the press and the public. Then, to challenge the Bama players even further, the few times practice was open, for instance when the visiting sportswriters came to town, they reverted to their old pro set to throw the writers off the scent. It was complete subterfuge. When the visitors left, they secured the perimeter and returned to practicing the wishbone.

Bryant later explained why he was so convinced this offense would work. "This system is great for a team that doesn't have a great drop-back passer," Bryant said. "We had the best in Trammell, Namath, Stabler, Sloan, and Hunter, but now we didn't have the kind of back I needed."

Surely Bryant didn't mean to diminish the abilities of quarterback Terry Davis. In fact, he further explained that with this offense, the quarterback has to be your best athlete since he has to very quickly judge whether to pass or to run.

In other words, adapt.

As the Bama players quickly learned, the wishbone, so named for the shape in which the backs line up, is a formation designed for running and passing on a roll. Basically, it's a triple-option ground offense where the quarterback looks to both his fullback and his trailing halfback.

"The wishbone is not hard to teach, but it's a very disciplined offense," Coach Gryska explained. "Everyone has to know what everyone else is doing. It's about execution. The players took to it real well. Once we had it down we were back to contact football."

Photo courtesy of the Paul W. Bryant Museum, the University of Alabama.

All-American halfback Johnny Musso.

So, during the clandestine practices before the '71 season, the players got busy learning their new blocking assignments and running the new system. Johnny Musso, the star tailback who had already distinguished himself on the 1970 squad, later told a reporter he was skeptical of the wishbone at first.

"Here it was three weeks before the opener with Southern Cal, and Coach walks into the squad meeting and says we're going to put away the passing game and put in the wishbone," Musso said.

Nonetheless, as Gryska said, Musso and his teammates took to the wishbone immediately. It was a very difficult offense for other teams to defend against, especially if the other teams they played were not running the wishbone.

As the opening game approached, incredibly Bama had managed to keep its secret weapon under wraps. At this point, the coaches knew they would have to let the broadcast crew in on the wishbone so they would be able to describe the plays. So John Forney, the Voice of the Tide, color analyst Doug Layton, and sideline reporter Jerry Duncan were all called into an underground meeting where the coaches explained the new offense. Of course they were sworn to absolute secrecy—they were told not even to tell their families.

So after one final dramatic night practice, which Bryant called to simulate the night game Bama would be playing in California, the team traveled to Los Angeles for their September rematch with USC. Every sportswriter had picked Southern Cal to win. Some had the Trojans favored by eleven points, others by as much as three touchdowns.

John Forney told the story of arriving in town for the traditional pregame media luncheon and running into the play-by-play man from Southern Cal, a guy he was friendly with, who asked him, "What's new?"

Now, it's very common for broadcasters from opposing teams, many of whom are friends, to share information. We don't give anything away that would hurt our team or betray the confidence of a coach, but before a game we might tip off a colleague to "watch the fullback" or "make sure you know who's under center all the time" without giving away the whole story.

So the USC guy asked John, "What's new?" And John said, "Oh, nothing." The guy pressed further. "Any injuries?" Nope. "How are the new players doing?" Fine.

John said he had to blatantly lie to the man and felt awful about it. When the game began and Bama's broadcast crew launched into an eloquent description of what was going on, John said, "I looked over to my left and saw the play-by-play guy from Southern Cal staring daggers at me. He was so teed off!" But Forney had no choice. Coach Bryant would have tarred and feathered him if he had given even a hint of what was to come.

So, Bama rolled into the USC game and emerged from their proverbial crimson-colored Trojan horse. They stunned their opponents from the first play and on the first drive, Johnny Musso, "the Italian Stallion," went in for a touchdown. Bama put up ten unanswered points before the half was over.

The Trojans did score ten points in the second half but it wasn't enough. Bama won it, 17-10. The wishbone was a smash.

Musso, who was given the game ball, graciously turned it over to Coach Bryant, who just happened to be marking his two hundredth win.

"You deserve it, Coach," Musso said.

Alabama kept putting the polish on their new offense that year, and went on to win eleven in a row. A big loss to Nebraska in the Orange Bowl marred an otherwise perfect record. But no doubt about it, Bama was back.

The 1972 season was a near-perfect repeat of 1971. Bama had the wishbone down. Until the heartbreaking 17-16 loss to Auburn at season's end, there seemed to be no stopping them. Despite the loss (the infamous "Punt, Bama, Punt!" game), Bama still took the SEC championship home to Tuscaloosa. But there was one more setback that season, in the form of a 17-13 loss to none other than the University of Texas in the Cotton Bowl on New Year's Day.

If someone had to beat the Tide, it might as well have been Darrell Royal's seventh-ranked Longhorns. The "student," however legendary, couldn't quite beat the "teacher." Even with his No. 3-ranked team. Not this time.

Bama took the early lead. After a stunning thirty-one-yard scoring run by Wilbur Jackson, the Tide was on top, 10-0. The offense, led by the blocking of Big John Hannah, racked up 324 yards, but the Longhorns surged ahead and ultimately won this "Battle of the Wishbones," 17-13.

We can only imagine what was said on the hotline that night.

In 1973 Bama redeemed itself by winning its ninth national championship (UPI), the fourth for Bear Bryant. (Note: this was actually a split title since Notre Dame won from everyone except UPI and a service called Dunkel, which gave Oklahoma the nod.) Any talk of a slump was over and at this point, no one was questioning the success of the wishbone. Except maybe for some of the players. Privately, of course.

Gary Rutledge, who shared quarterbacking duties with Richard Todd to great acclaim during 1973, remembers his first wishbone experience while playing backup quarterback to Terry Davis in '72.

"My first play ever at Alabama was my sophomore year," Rutledge said. "It was the first game of the year, and I really wasn't expecting to go in. I was over there sitting on my helmet, pretty much. Well, they had those tearaway jerseys then, and Terry Davis was trotting off the field with his jersey torn. All of the sudden, they were hollering, 'Rutledge! Rutledge! Get in here!'

"Well, Coach (Mal) Moore gets me on the sideline and says, 'Gary, run a right counter, forty-nine option.' That's the hardest wishbone play ever, where you fake to the right, reverse out and turn your back to the defensive end, and pitch it outside. It's my first varsity play and he makes me run the hardest one. I reverse out, the end luckily is not coming at me hard. I run out there and pitch it on the ground. Well, I'm trotting back off the field because Terry is coming back on. So I went running over to Coach Moore and Coach Bryant expecting to get chewed out, reamed out really bad. But then, Coach Bryant just looks at me and says, 'Gary, I just want to apologize for Mal for calling that play.'"

"Yeah, I got a lot of advice," laughed Moore, who was quarterbacks coach under Bryant and currently serves as Alabama's athletic director. "Coach Bryant would needle me about throwing. We didn't throw the ball a lot when we would run the wishbone. He liked misdirection stuff. He thought the wishbone was too much of a flow offense; it was easy for the left-side linebacker. He'd say, 'Mal, we are making an all-American out of every linebacker we play. We need more counter options, misdirection reverses.'

"So, we were playing the University of Houston when the split-back veer was at its height. We would score, they would score. We couldn't ever quite get away from them. They punted in the fourth quarter, dead on just about our eight-yard-line. I am trying to get it off the goal line because we can still lose the game. I call a play. Coach Bryant says, 'Gosh, Mal, the backside line-backer made the play; run a reverse.' I'm thinking run a reverse down here, it's either a big play or big loss, no in-between. We call another play and pop it out ten or fifteen yards, first down. He said, 'The backside linebacker is killing you. Run the reverse.'

"I call another play with another big gain with a fullback. We are out about midfield. It's first and ten. He grabs my arm. I could tell when he meant what he said. We locked eyes. He said, 'Run the reverse.' So I went left, thirty-six, low, wide reverse. We ride that fullback deal back to the wide receiver. Houston's big ol' end was 'give out'; he didn't pursue. You know, he sees it and comes up the field. We lose about fifteen yards. They hit the ground right in front of Coach and me. We were both backing up. Coach Bryant looked at me and said, 'Damn it, I meant the other way!'"

Bryant liked to switch directions. He was full of surprises. Just like the wishbone, he kept his options open. Players from different eras tell similar stories of how the coach would surprise them by taking full blame for a loss, which they never expected him to do. Then he would turn around and punish the team after they won, sometimes by a lot, if he didn't think it was done in the right way.

Bryant, the man, was a contradiction. But as much as we think of him as tough and never wavering, it's evident so much of his success came from his ability to change and adapt.

Part of it was the wisdom that comes with age, but later in his career he would say things you never thought you would have heard him say.

"I think he got a little more lovable towards the players the last few years of his career," Coach Gryska said. "He'd say, 'If I can't love ya, I don't want ya!' Now, in the sixties if a man said, 'I love ya,' to another man, he might have run out the door."

This was the same man who in 1958 told his new players, "I don't know you, and I don't want to know you. After spring practice I'll decide who I want to know."

Bryant employed the wishbone, in one form or another until he retired in 1982. This kind of offense, always uniquely a college football animal and primarily a weapon of southern teams, is not seen so much anymore (although Bama, under head coach Mike Shula, did resurrect "the Bone" for three or four plays against Auburn in the 2004 Iron Bowl).

Even though it's on the endangered list, Coach Gene Stallings said the wishbone is still a workable offense.

"You've got to have a quarterback that can make that right decision of giving the ball to the fullback, keeping it, or pitching it," he said. "The thing about the wishbone, though, is if you get behind, it's kind of hard to catch up. You can't be a good passing team and a good wishbone team."

The reason we don't see the wishbone in the pros? Coach Stallings explains: "If you paid $5 million for your quarterback would you want him keeping the football on the option or throwing the pass?"

The option offense that is used by so many college teams today is an offshoot of the wishbone. The formations are different but the ideas are basically the same. Times have changed and football had to change, too.

But oh, what a thing it was.

FOURTEEN

The '78 Championship— Goal Line Stand

Gut Checks All Around

IF YOU HAD TO PICK JUST THREE WORDS TO SUM UP ALABAMA football, they would be: *Goal Line Stand.*

Say these three words and Alabama fans everywhere are instantly transported to a moment that will forever define the grit, the fortitude, the dedication, and the can-do attitude of the Crimson Tide. It all happened at the Sugar Bowl on January 1, 1979, when Alabama played Penn State for the 1978 national title.

The pressure was on. Going into this game, Penn State (11-0) was ranked No. 1 and Alabama (10-1) was ranked No. 2. Before the game a reporter, who should have known better, asked Coach Bryant if he had asked for Penn State coach Joe Paterno's vote in the coaches' top twenty poll.

"No, I didn't!" Bryant growled. "And I wouldn't ask for yours."

The crowd at the Superdome in New Orleans was supercharged, not to mention the millions of folks watching at home. The winner of this game would take all.

The first three quarters were by no means boring, but the fourth quarter was an absolute thriller. Bama was up, 14-7, when it fumbled at its own nineteen yard line. Penn State recovered and successfully moved the ball into scoring position inside the Alabama one yard line. Penn State quarterback Chuck Fusina had hit receiver Scott Fitzkee for a five-yard completion that would have given the Lions their six points had it not been for Bama's Don McNeal who made a touchdown-saving tackle inside the Alabama one.

Penn State could have scored right then and we wouldn't be having this discussion. But McNeal made the great tackle. No score.

Third down. Penn State is inside the Alabama one yard line again, just inches away. The Lions sent Matt Suhey diving over the top, but he ran smack-dab into Bama linebacker Rich Wingo, a great defender. Wingo was a magnificent physical specimen who later went on to be a strength and conditioning coach at Bama and at other schools. He liked to hit, and he leapt up and went straight for Suhey, just short of the goal line.

Fourth and goal. Still, one yard to go. If Penn State scores, they're going to win the national title. If Alabama stops them, the Tide's going to win it. That whole year, all of the buildup and all of the respect between these two schools—it was always a very respectful, healthy rivalry—came down to this moment. Think about it. Bear Bryant is standing on one sideline and across the field stands the legendary Joe Paterno. One play to go. Incredible.

While Fusina had a quick conference with Paterno, the Bama defenders had a little end-zone meeting of their own.

"We get back in the huddle, fourth down and inches, and we all held hands," All-American linebacker Barry Krauss said. "It was just everything we wanted and prayed about. That's what you want. I mean, you want it on the line. With Coach Bryant, this was the way it was supposed to happen. So when they came out, we didn't know if they were going to run a pass, a sweep, whatever."

As Penn State came to the line of scrimmage, Bama tackle Marty Lyons took this moment to offer Penn State a little friendly advice. "Chuck (Fusina) just looked at me and he says, 'What do you think we should do?'" Lyons remembered. "I said, 'I think you should throw the ball.'"

This piece of advice has morphed into a Bama catchphrase over the years. Again, three little words: *You better pass.*

Enough talk. The Bama defenders lined up shoulder to shoulder. "I was scared to death they were going to fake a dive and go outside," Krauss said.

They didn't. Fusina handed off to tailback Mike Guman, who went straight up the middle. Krauss and company were there to stop him.

"It's kind of like we had to do whatever it took to get it done," Krauss said. "It was a real gut check."

Everything happened so fast. At the same time, the moment seemed to

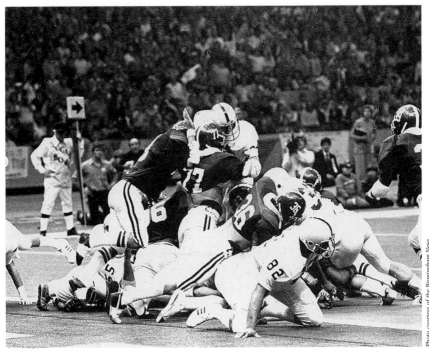

The Goal Line Stand.

last forever. Krauss says he simply hit Guman as hard as he could. Bama safety Murray Legg came along to further reinforce the hit. The rest of the two teams then piled on.

"I really didn't do much," Krauss said. "But when I hit him, I pinched a nerve in my neck and I actually broke a chip off my helmet! I was just kind of holding him when Murray Legg pushed us over."

From the bottom of this pile of bodies, Krauss says he heard roars from the crowd but didn't know what that meant. Who was yelling? The people in crimson and white or the guys in blue and white? Then Marty Lyons stepped in, picked Krauss up, and said, "We finally did it. We won the national championship!"

After this classic game and classic play that would be forever burned in the memory of college football fans, the results were in. Despite Bama's win, the polls were split. Southern Cal, who had beaten Bama earlier in the year, won the UPI/Coaches poll. But the AP sportswriters/sportscasters poll gave it to Alabama. So, even though they had to share, Bama had their title.

Coach Bryant declared his choice, "I will proudly cast my vote for Alabama because today I think we have the best football team in America."

To this day Barry Krauss and Marty Lyons completely light up when telling the story of the Goal Line Stand. More than twenty-five years later you can see the fire burning in their eyes when they talk about it. Obviously, this victory meant more to their lives (both went on to NFL careers) than they ever could have imagined.

"It's your dream when you play at the University of Alabama to have a chance to play the number-one-ranked team in the country," Krauss said. "Especially those of us who were seniors (who) went into that game knowing it meant a lot. But I had no idea how much people would remember that one play! I think it affected me when I ended up being drafted by the Colts so early. But as Coach Bryant always told us, it was all about team. Lots of guys had big plays in that game."

Don McNeal, who pulled off one of the biggest plays, also never imagined the impact that simply doing his job would have on himself as well as thousands of Alabama fans.

"I was just playing football," McNeal said. "I didn't know it was a big play at the time. But it was one of the bigger plays of my life."

Rich Wingo, who also made a huge play, virtually echoes his teammates sentiments. "Here's a moment you dream about happening," Wingo said, "and here it was staring at us in the face. Gut-check time. Coach always preached it, jaw-to-jaw, cheek-to-cheek. They weren't going anywhere."

It was gut-check time all around.

"I think it was a great team effort," Marty Lyons said. "We had a great coaching staff. We were well prepared going into the game. For those of us who had a chance to play for a guy like (defensive coordinator) Ken Donahue, he would be there night after night, day after day, running the tapes over and over and over again. It was like a religion to him. For the defensive linemen, we owe a lot to Coach Donahue. He pushed us to our limits."

The fabulously successful 1978 season didn't come out of nowhere. It was Coach Bryant's twenty-first year as head coach. After weathering some major ups and downs, this coach and this team felt another championship season was long overdue.

With apologies to Charles Dickens, the decade leading up to 1978 was the best of times and the worst of times for Alabama football. After winning national championships in 1964 and 1965, things slipped a bit for the Tide. During the late sixties, especially during the off-season of 1969, where Bama went just 6-5. In 1969 Coach Bryant was heard to say things like, "We have not been hitting people the way you are supposed to when wearing that red jersey," or even more definitive comments such as, "We are piss-poor."

Things weren't much better in 1970. Despite boasting great players such as quarterback Scott Hunter, all-American tailback Johnny Musso, and guard John Hannah, who would be named all-American the very next year, in 1970 the Crimson Tide barely squeaked out a "winning" season. They finished 6-5-1. The tone this year was set by the season opener where Southern Cal's star, Sam Cunningham ran all over the Tide's defense, scoring three touchdowns in the Trojans' 42-21 win.

Things turned around for the Tide in 1971 when Bryant introduced the Wishbone offense to great success. In very dramatic form, he sprung his new, until then top-secret offense, on Southern Cal and Bama took its revenge by winning that year's game, 17-10. Bama crushed the rest of their opponents that year and won the SEC championship, only to lose to Nebraska in the Orange Bowl.

The 1973 team, led by quarterbacks Richard Todd and Gary Rutledge, stacked up an incredible 477 points, still a school record for most points scored in a single season. The Tide lost to Notre Dame in the Sugar Bowl (24-23) but still came up with a split-decision national title (shared with the Fighting Irish).

In 1974 and '75, the Tide again won the SEC championship, but missed winning the conference title in 1976, when they finished just 9-3—(remember, this is Alabama! The bar is high!) Then, in 1977, Bama was back as SEC champs. The terrific season was capped off by a Sugar Bowl win against Ohio State (35-6). The press made a big to-do out of this game, framing it as a battle between two legendary coaches, Bear Bryant and the Buckeyes' Woody Hayes.

In customary form, Bryant tried to dilute that angle: "I don't know why you people keep making such a big deal over Woody Hayes and Paul Bryant," he said. "I assure you I'm not going to play, and I hope Woody does."

After Bama won the game, Bryant planted his tongue in his cheek when reporters asked his opinion of the famous Coach Hayes: "Woody's a great coach. But I ain't bad."

In 1977 Alabama just missed the national championship after Notre Dame beat No. 1 Texas in the Cotton Bowl. So close . . .

Nineteen seventy-eight was a stellar year for the Crimson Tide. Combined with the powerful repeat national championship season of 1979, this period would define the last of Bear Bryant's great teams. True, he would go on to coach three more wonderful years and 1981 would mark the milestone whereby Bryant became the winningest college football coach of all time. But we have to stop right here and acknowledge that the '78 and '79 teams were something truly special.

In 1979 Alabama swept its opponents for twelve straight victories. The statistics that year were staggering. Bama made twenty-eight first downs against Georgia Tech, kept the ball for ninety-three plays against Baylor, gained six hundred yards against Vandy, and held Florida to just three first downs. They beat Arkansas in the Sugar Bowl, 24-9.

Bama counted three All-Americans on its '79 roster: tackle Jim Bunch, cornerback Don McNeal, and center Dwight Stephenson. As it has been noted many times before, Coach Bryant was not a man to gush, but regarding Stephenson he said, "Stephenson was a man among children. He didn't say very much but he didn't have to. He was the best center I've ever coached."

Dwight Stephenson at center.

Photo courtesy of the Paul W. Bryant Museum, the University of Alabama.

John Hannah never played with Stephenson at Alabama, but sought inspiration from him when they both later played in the NFL.

"There is no better center that ever played the game than Dwight," Hannah said. "I played with a lot of good centers but Dwight is the best. As a matter of fact, I got killed in a game against Chicago once because of him. I watched Dwight get up under Refrigerator Perry and flip him.

Perry would go on his back! So, I went out there and tried to flip the Refrigerator and the only person who got flipped was me! I had to go back to my own style."

Stephenson returns the compliment, telling a story about a game when his Miami Dolphins met Hannah's New England Patriots.

"I consider John to be the greatest offensive lineman that ever played the game," Stephenson said. "Our whole defense was set up for John Hannah and the way he came off the football. We designed our plays just for him! The way he did it was just amazing."

Stephenson, an NFL Hall of Famer, has even more compliments for his Alabama brethren. In 1980, one of his Dolphins teammates was former Bama defensive tackle Bob Baumhower.

"Some of the things I learned to do in the NFL were out of trying not to be embarrassed," Stephenson said. "I had to go against Bob Baumhower in practice every day and I hated it. Then, finally one day I figured out how to play Bob Baumhower. He gets very, very, very close to my face, right? I had a free hand, you know, the centers do. He would get real close and be ready to come off the football. I just pushed his head down and he hit the ground. He said, 'Dwight, you hurt me, man.' So I did it a couple of times. All of a sudden, he adjusted his stance. He sat back a little bit and then I could get underneath him and that's what I was trying to do the whole time. I learned that by practicing against Bob, who was no question one of the best defensive linemen ever to play at Alabama or in the NFL."

Even in the NFL—whether playing on the same or opposing teams—it seems the Bama bond cannot be broken. Broadcasting NFL games on the radio on Sundays as I do now, I'll run into many, many former Bama players. We'll talk down on the field before the games or in the locker room after the game and all they want is the "inside scoop" on what's the latest at the Capstone. Marty Lyons, now a broadcaster for the New York Jets, ran into me—get this—at the buffet table in the press room at Gillette Stadium in Foxborough, Massachusetts, during the 2004 season. He and I got together, and just hours before a huge NFL battle of the unbeatens (the Jets and the Patriots, both at 5-0) we sat there talking Bama football.

For the guys who have Bear Bryant in common, the connection seems to be even deeper. As I've mentioned before, former players still talk about Bryant to this day.

Whether the setting was a Sugar Bowl game at the Superdome or Bryant-Denny Field during an afternoon spring practice, every Bama player at one point or another experienced what Coach Bryant called a "gut-check." And often, even with the players who turned out to be the biggest stars, the gut-check involved the huge decision of whether or not to quit.

Joe Namath went through it. So did Kenny Stabler, Bob Baumhower, and even Barry Krauss. It was during the 1976 season and Bama had just won a game.

Touchdown Alabama!

Photo courtesy of the Paul W. Bryant Museum, the University of Alabama.

"We came back to Birmingham and had a special meeting," Krauss said. "We had just won the game, 56-0, or something like that. Coach Bryant said, 'You guys disgust me.' Basically he said forget about playing any more football because this is not the way Alabama football should be played. Anyway, this was my sophomore year and I felt like I was doing everything I could to play for Alabama and it just wasn't working out.

"So, I went out with my roommate and we decided, forget it. We're not playing at Alabama. Who cares, right? Now, in the four years I played, Coach Bryant checked curfew one night. Guess what night I was out?"

Krauss, terrified of getting kicked off the team went to his buddy Marty Lyons for advice. "I'd hate to be you," Lyons said.

Krauss decided he had no choice but to face Coach Bryant. He mustered all his courage and went to the coach's office and took his place on the now legendary sofa, which former players report was notoriously low to the ground, especially in relation to the coach's sturdy oak desk, which loomed above eye level.

"You sink in that dang sofa," Krauss said. "So I jumped back up. I'm standing in front of Coach Bryant. I said, 'I'm sorry for missing curfew. I just felt like I wanted an opportunity to play for you but you're not giving it to me.' He had his head down. He wasn't looking at me."

At this defining moment in his life, what did Krauss do?

"I started crying," he said. "And when he still wasn't looking at me, I took crying to a whole other level. I started jerking all over. Told him if I lost my scholarship my mom would kill me. Finally, he mumbled something. I think it was, 'Son, you better straighten up.' Well, my roommate did not go see Coach Bryant and he got kicked out of the dorm. I stayed. And I learned something. When you're in a lot of trouble, cry."

And two years later, Krauss would hardly be able to hold back the tears as Alabama celebrated his championship-inducing Goal Line Stand, a play that will forever define what Alabama football is all about.

FIFTEEN

The Iron Bowl

The War Between the State

SAY THE NAME "LEGION FIELD" AND MEMORIES FLOOD OVER Alabama football fans. So many wonderful plays. Too many to count. But of all the great, game-making moments, only one has the distinction of being voted by the fans as the most important play in the history of Legion Field. That honor belongs to Van Tiffin and his fifty-two-yard field goal in the final seconds to beat the Auburn Tigers in 1985.

"As a kicker, you want the opportunity to make a last-second field goal," Tiffin said. "That's a dream any kicker would have. But you don't want it to be fifty-two yards!"

Van Tiffin.

Photo courtesy of the Paul W. Bryant Museum, the University of Alabama.

The play was named best-ever because it was an astounding, pressure-packed, and very long kick. It also took the prize because it came at the conclusion of a very emotional and exciting football game. But the play was voted "best" mainly because it resulted in a win against Auburn.

No doubt, if that kick had won the Louisiana Tech game, people would have said, "Way to go, man," and that would have been the end of it. Van Tiffin probably wouldn't be retelling the story over and over again and signing autographs when people come to look at RVs at his family's place of business, Tiffin Motorhomes, in Red Bay, Alabama.

It's all about Auburn.

Inside the state of Alabama, there is nothing more important than the annual Alabama-Auburn game. Up until 1989, when the teams met for the first time at Jordan-Hare Stadium in Auburn, the game, referred to as "the Iron Bowl," was played at Legion Field in Birmingham in order to accommodate the huge number of fans who wanted to attend. Each university got half the tickets, and the game was played on neutral territory. The *Iron* in "Iron Bowl" refers to the fact that Birmingham boasted large amounts of iron ore in nearby mountains, making it at one time "the Steel City of the South."

These days, the yearly matchup takes place at each school's respective stadiums, which have both been expanded. This makes for a much more exciting backdrop. The years we suffer all that orange and blue on the Auburn campus are worth it the next season when we play in Tuscaloosa and the crowd is 95 percent crimson and white.

Coach Gene Stallings, who coached at Texas A&M before he came to Bama, perfectly explained what this rivalry means to Alabamians: "Talk about the Texas-Texas A&M game will start a week before the game and continue for a week after," he said, "but talk about the Alabama-Auburn game never stops. You can go to any drugstore or any restaurant and they're talking about the game year-round. Alabama-Auburn is the greatest rivalry I've ever been associated with."

While he was Alabama's head coach, Coach Ray Perkins noted that, "More people in Alabama care passionately about it (Auburn-Alabama) than the Super Bowl."

This is absolutely true. Part of the reason that other in-state college rivalries around the country may not be as intense as Alabama-Auburn is that most states have enough distractions to

Coach Gene Stallings.

Photo courtesy of Kent Gidley, the University of Alabama.

dilute their passion. Michigan State–Michigan is a hot one but folks in Michigan have the Detroit Tigers, the Lions, the Pistons, and the Red Wings to compete for their attention. USC and UCLA is big, but they've got the Dodgers and the Angels, the Lakers and the Clippers, not to mention Disneyland and the beach, to help occupy their thoughts. In Alabama, college football is the major league sport and Alabama-Auburn is the Super Bowl and World Series all rolled into one. If you grow up in Alabama, from the time you can crawl, you'd better pick a side.

Van Tiffin knew what side he was on that day in November 1985, when he was summoned for his last-minute kick. The thing was, he thought he would be staying on the sidelines. He didn't think he'd be going in.

"There were two drunk guys in the stadium hollering, 'Hey! It's gonna all come down to you!'" Tiffin recalled. "But I didn't worry about it because it wasn't looking too good."

Indeed, after trailing almost the entire game, Auburn, led by none other than Heisman Trophy winner and eventual multisport superstar Bo Jackson, had pulled ahead, 23-22, with under a minute left! Mike Shula, quarterback of the 1985 squad (and Bama's future head coach), remembers those final ticking moments as if they happened this morning.

"We went back and forth all during the fourth quarter. Then we came up with a fourth-and-four play," Shula said, "We called a reverse, executed it, and made the first down. I think we had one or two plays left. The first play was incomplete and the second play seemed like it took forever because they were only rushing three guys, and it didn't look like anybody was open. Finally, one of our receivers came open across the middle and we hit him for a completion."

Paul Kennedy, who was doing the radio play-by-play that day, was yelling on-the-air to Bama's Greg Richardson, who obviously couldn't hear him, "Get out of bounds! Get out of bounds!"

Richardson did in fact drag the Auburn defender out of bounds. The clock stopped with seven seconds left and Shula left the field completely exhausted.

Enter Tiffin, who didn't even have time to get nervous.

"We were in the hurry-up field goal there," Tiffin said. "That was good because there wasn't a lot of time to think and ponder on it."

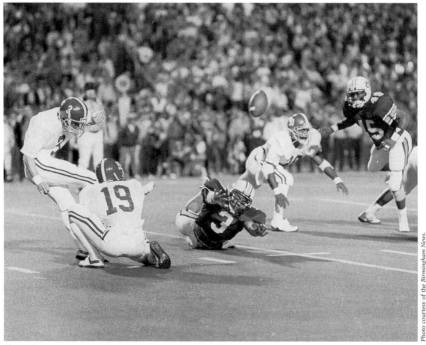

The Kick.

He nailed the kick, an incredible fifty-two yards, and Alabama won, 25-23. The fans and players rushed onto the field and mobbed Tiffin.

"I'm one of the slowest guys on the team, but that day I was the first one to the kicker!" Shula said.

Kermit Kendrick, who was a freshman on the team, backs Shula's claim. "That was the only time Mike Shula beat Wes Neighbors running!" Kendrick said.

To this day, Tiffin is incredibly self-effacing about this life-changing event, which wasn't just luck. Tiffin was named all-American in 1986. He still holds the school record for a fifty-seven-yarder he made against Texas A&M in 1985. And, it just so happened he hit another fifty-two-yarder against Auburn the previous year. But this is the one we remember.

Everybody has heard of Van Tiffin (aka "Ol' Thunderfoot"), yet I find it funny that nobody *knows* him. Before our pregame show prior to the 2004 Iron Bowl, I was walking with our engineer/producer Tom Stipe from Bryant-Denny Stadium to the Quad. Tom and I were admiring the sights and sounds of big-time SEC football. Then, midway through our stroll, as we neared Denny Chimes, approaching from the other direction was this smallish man, wearing a plaid shirt, walking by himself, speaking to and being noticed by no one. As we passed each other, amidst thousands of avid Bama fans, I said to this man, "Hi, Van. Great to see you." His response included a few words and a quick smile. There I was, chatting ever so briefly with the man voted as making the biggest play ever for the University of Alabama at Legion Field, and the assembled masses offered not a glimmer of recognition to this man in the plaid shirt.

ONE REASON THE IRON BOWL IS SO IMPORTANT TO ALABAMA FANS is the fact that historical events have a habit of taking place there. The milestones are many.

Dennis Riddle notches six more for the good guys.

Photo courtesy of Kent Gidley, the University of Alabama.

Arguably, *the* milestone in the annals of Alabama football was marked during the 1981 Iron Bowl. After Bama emerged victorious (final score 28-17), Coach Paul "Bear" Bryant claimed his 315th career coaching victory, making him the all-time-winningest coach in Division I-A history.

At the start of the 1981 season, people had been acutely aware that Bryant was approaching this record, originally held by Coach Amos Alonzo Stagg. Fans and media types talked about it constantly. There was little doubt he would break the record. It was just a matter of when.

It took a little longer than Bryant might have liked. The quest for the record was psyching up Bama's opponents, resulting in some unwanted losses for the Crimson and White. No team wanted to be the team that delivered the Bear his record.

After Bryant tied the record with his 314th win (31-16) against Penn State, only Auburn remained on Bama's regular schedule.

On November 28 the two teams met for their annual Legion Field extravaganza. The Tigers were the underdog that year, but they provided plenty of drama by pulling ahead of the Tide, 17-14, during the third quarter. In the fourth quarter Bama had gone back ahead, 21-17, when halfback Linnie Patrick took off on a spectacular thirty-one-yard sprint that ended just shy of Auburn's goal line.

Patrick, a sophomore who had spent more than his share of time in Bryant's proverbial doghouse for offenses both on and off the field, basically redeemed himself in this moment. The word *remarkable* doesn't begin to describe this run.

Quarterback Walter Lewis pitched the ball to Patrick, who was hit and almost hit again and again by scads of Auburn defenders. At one point he was even hopping on one foot but the man would not go down. Eventually, he landed back on earth, some thirty-one yards later. Poetic justice was done when Linnie later scored the Tide's final touchdown, ending the game and sealing the deal for Coach Bryant with the 28-17 victory.

"That was one of the greatest runs I have ever seen," said Bryant, who was not one to gush.

"It was a great, great game," said Patrick, who was enjoying the best moment of his college career. "Beating Auburn is always special. But getting the record for Coach Bryant made it even more so."

Bryant's teams had many great victories against Auburn during his twenty-five-year run as Bama's head coach. Alabama lost to Auburn in 1958, Bryant's first season, but after that, they wouldn't lose again until 1963. Alabama-Auburn watchers love to keep track of stats like these. Four wins in a row? Not too shabby. But for those of you scoring at home, here's something really incredible—during those same four years, 1959–1962, not only did Bama win, but they didn't allow Auburn to score one single point against them! Not one!

Billy Neighbors, who played tackle on three of those teams, still beams when he thinks of that accomplishment.

"Auburn never scored on us!" Neighbors said. "One year, our goal was to keep them from getting across their own forty, because they had a great field-goal kicker. And they didn't even do that. It really makes those Auburn people mad!"

There have been more than a few blowouts over the years. In fact Bama has left the Tigers scoreless fourteen times in the history of this rivalry. But there's something about the close ones that we remember even more.

On everyone's short list of Bama's best all-time plays is quarterback Kenny "the Snake" Stabler's famous Run in the Mud on December 2, 1967. It was the wettest, muddiest, nastiest of days—not exactly conducive to long pass plays or any type of play where one needed to remain for the most part, upright.

As expected, Coach Bryant told Stabler not to throw the football. This sloppy game would be all about running and taking advantage of the other guy's mistakes. Then, when Auburn was up by three in the fourth quarter, the Snake made his move. He called an option, saw a hole, and plowed through it on a forty-seven-yard run for a touchdown. Bama won, 7-3, and the Run in the Mud was entered into Alabama legend.

Snake rallies the troops during an Iron Bowl.

"Coming up through the ranks, we all

heard these stories of the Alabama-Auburn rivalry," Stabler said. "Then, as a player when you walk in the footsteps of Gilmer, Trammel, and Namath, you just want to beat Auburn. It's as simple as that."

Would Stabler still be retelling that story in our broadcast booth before Alabama games or out and about in Tuscaloosa the night before homecoming if he hadn't completed that thrilling run in a game-winning play against Auburn? Maybe. But the fact that it was against Auburn guaranteed he will be telling that story for life.

All-American Johnny Musso, who now lives in Chicago, still gets asked about Auburn. But at least Musso doesn't have to recount the same play over and over. During the famous 1971 game, in which Bama routed Auburn, 31-7, Musso ran for 167 yards and two touchdowns on thirty-three carries. So, when fans say, "Hey, Johnny. Tell us about that great play against Auburn," Musso has to ask, "Which one?"

The 1971 matchup was one of Coach Bryant's all-time favorite victories. After the game, in which Bama held Auburn quarterback and Heisman Trophy winner Pat Sullivan to his lowest output of yardage, Coach Bryant said, "I know one thing. I'd rather die now than to have died and missed this game."

Quarterback Gary Rutledge.

Photo courtesy of the Paul W. Bryant Museum, the University of Alabama.

Gary Rutledge, who played quarterback for the Tide from 1972 to 1974, is asked to tell his Auburn story just about every other day. "In 1972, I was backup quarterback against Auburn. That was the year they blocked our kicks and beat us, 17-16. They even had those bumper stickers that said, 'Punt, Bama, Punt!' So, the next year, in '73, we go 10–0, and it comes time to play Auburn. Well, this really means something to the coaches, to Coach Bryant. You could see it in the preparation that week before. So, we beat them, 35-0. After that whipping we gave them, the new bumper stickers said, 'Score, Auburn, Score!'"

Photo courtesy of the Paul W. Bryant Museum, the University of Alabama.

Steadman Shealy leads the 1979 Crimson Tide to a 25-18 win over Auburn.

Steadman Shealy, Bama's quarterback from 1977 to 1979, played in three Iron Bowls, but the game he's always asked to recount is the 1979 thriller. The Crimson Tide, ranked No. 1 in the nation, had been heavily favored to win. But after a series of fumbles and mishaps, Bama was shocked to find itself down, 18-17, in the fourth quarter.

Refusing to quit, Bama got it together during its next possession and plowed down the field, all the way to the eight. First and goal.

"We called 'Thirty-seven Option,'" Shealy said. "Just plain triple option. The defense would determine who got the ball."

So, Shealy ran the option. When a defender moved to cover Major Ogilvie, who was the trailing back, Shealy burst through the middle and scored. Bama won, 25-18, and Shealy had his story of a lifetime.

My favorite Iron Bowl story is from 1989, when Bama traveled to Auburn to play at Jordan-Hare Stadium for the first time. The anticipation was unbearable. The buildup was unbelievable. The Tide spent the night before the game at a hotel in Montgomery. Judging by the number of TV cameras and reporters camped out outside, you would have thought President Reagan and Mikhail Gorbachev were inside negotiating a nuclear arms reduction agreement. This was big.

Jim Fyffe was the longtime "Voice" of the Auburn Tigers and a great friend of mine. We had talked earlier in the week, and since I didn't really know my way around Auburn very well, we agreed to ride to the stadium together in his car. So, off we went. The "Voice" of the Tide and the "Voice" of the Tigers, in the same car, down I-85 towards the Wire Road exit in Auburn.

People from other vehicles kept looking into Jim's car, spotting us riding together. Eli and Jim . . . Jim and Eli . . . The Tide and the Tigers. It was blowing people's minds.

When we arrived at the stadium and emerged from the same car, you would've thought the world had ended. The reactions to that sight were priceless. Jim and I just smiled. I waved to the Auburn fans. He waved toward the Bama fans. Folks didn't know what to think.

When we arrived at our respective broadcast booths, it was early—the quiet before the storm on this historic day. I dropped off my stuff then went over to the Auburn booth to sit with Jim and while away the hours. We talked and read the morning paper.

Later, Jim's wife, Rose, a woman with whom I have always had a good relationship, walked into the Auburn booth to check in with her husband. As she was leaving she looked back over her shoulder and said, "See you later, Sweetheart." Before Jim could react I said, "OK, see you later." The look that Rose gave me that morning can still chill a summer's afternoon. The thought of this still brings a smile to my face.

Thankfully, my offbeat comment didn't ruin our friendship. I don't know Rose well, but what I know, I like.

For years afterward, I looked forward to the time when my path would cross with Jim's. We would catch up often by phone. Oddly enough, even though we did talk Alabama-Auburn football, we really only occasionally talked about sports. Usually we talked about our families, or we'd tell some raunchy jokes or just do what we did best—talk!

Sadly, a few years ago Jim passed away, all too young. What a loss.

Boy, how I miss Jim Fyffe.

WHEN IT COMES TO THE CELEBRATED AND ALWAYS HIGHLY ANTICIPATED Iron Bowls, there are so many stories. And since we're talking about football, every story has the requisite stats to go with it.

Story: After the scrappy 1907 tie between Auburn and Alabama, the teams didn't meet again for forty-one years.

Stat: Coach Red Drew, who led the '48 team (the year the series was revived), went on to best Auburn the next five years out of six.

Story: The 1999 Alabama victory over Auburn broke the Jordan-Hare Hex.

Stat: Alabama had gone nine years in a row without winning at Auburn's home stadium.

Story: The exciting combo of quarterback Andrew Zow and tailback Santonio Beard led Alabama to its exciting 2001 clobbering of Auburn.

Stat: This was the most lopsided win in the rivalry in nearly twenty-five years.

Story: Alabama vs. Auburn, America's top football rivalry.

Stat: At the end of the 2004 season, Alabama led the Iron Bowl tally to the tune of 39-33-1.

Story: So many more to come.

SIXTEEN

The Third Saturday in October

Too Much Damn Orange

FROM WHERE I SIT, THE BIGGEST PROBLEM WITH THE THIRD SATURDAY in October, the day Alabama traditionally plays Tennessee, is that there's just too much damn orange. But that's just my opinion. So, let's stick with an indisputable fact: The Alabama-Tennessee rivalry is among the most intense in all of college football.

Most Alabama players and fans count Auburn as their archrival. But some notch the Tennessee game just ahead of Auburn in terms of importance and bragging rights in the SEC. According to those closest to him, Coach Paul W. Bryant put Tennessee first on his hit list. The reasons may have been highly personal. To understand this, we have to go way, way back.

Before he was arguably the most famous college football coach that ever lived, Bryant was a football player for Alabama. In fact, during the 1935 season, a series of events would occur on the football field that would become as legendary as the famous bear-wrestling story that gave Bryant his better-known nickname.

By all accounts the 1935 season had gotten off to a shaky start. The Tide ended up with a disappointing tie after their first game against Howard (now Samford) University, a team they were expected to clobber. They beat George Washington, but then Mississippi State bested Bama 20-7. Worse, during the game Bryant fractured the shin bone on his right leg. When the team headed to Knoxville to face Tennessee the next week, Bryant had his leg in a cast and was walking on crutches. But before the game, the team doctor removed the cast and told him to go ahead and suit up, even if he wasn't going to play.

Then, defensive coach Hank Crisp used Bryant's situation to motivate the masses. "Hey, if this guy can tough it out on a broken leg . . ."

So when Coach Frank Thomas asked Bryant if he was ready to play, he felt he had no choice. So, he played. And he didn't just go through the motions and perform his duties in a perfunctory manner. He played the best game of his career! He set up two touchdowns, one by tossing a lateral to Riley Smith. He also caught a touchdown pass of his own. Bama whomped Tennessee, 25-0.

Sportswriters (being sportswriters), were skeptical of the story of the player with the broken leg.

Bert Bank, our producer emeritus at the Crimson Tide Sports Network, was a student at Alabama in 1935. "I remember very well when Bryant played with the broken leg," Bert said. "I don't think he played the whole game but everybody was talking about it!"

Bama's Charles Jones stops the Vols in their tracks.

The myth was put to print when Atlanta newspaperman Ralph McGill looked at the X-rays himself and wrote about it in his column. When asked about playing hurt, Bryant answered in the cowboy style he would later make famous, "It was just one little bone."

So the legend was born. Did playing in pain against Tennessee result in the proverbial bone Coach Bryant had against the Vols when he became head coach? Hard to say.

Coach Clem Gryska says the intensity of Bryant's focus on Tennessee went back to his time as head coach at the University of Kentucky.

"As a player at Alabama, he beat Tennessee. But at Kentucky, Coach Bryant never beat them," Gryska said. "He wanted them bad. We tied them his second season, in '59. Then in '61, we finally beat them. The Auburn game was incidental to Coach Bryant. He called Auburn 'that other school.' Tennessee was the big one."

No matter whether you ultimately describe the Bama-Tennessee matchup as the rivalry, no one can dispute the fact that every year, this is an exciting and incredibly highly charged football game. Intensifying the rivalry is the fact that since 1959, with the exception of just three years—1968, 1984, and 2000—at least one of the two teams has been nationally ranked every time they met. And, during thirteen of these years, both teams have been ranked.

Looking at these numbers, the rivalry makes even more sense. More often than not, there are national implications in an Alabama-Tennessee game. Not to mention a hot contest within the SEC.

THERE HAVE BEEN SO MANY UNFORGETTABLE ALABAMA-TENNESSEE contests they could fill a book. In fact, the late sports editor and writer Al Browning did write a fine book, *The Third Saturday in October*, which chronicled every matchup from the inaugural meeting on November 18, 1901—a tie game (7-7) that kept starting and stopping due to fans repeatedly taking to the field to fight—up through the 2000 game, which Alabama lost, 20-10, at Tennessee.

Since we're talking about Alabama-Tennessee, it should come as no surprise that perhaps the most memorable games are still to come. Certainly, the 2003 game is one for current and future books.

This game, played at Bryant-Denny Stadium and broadcast on CBS, was the longest game in the 111-year history of Alabama football. It was also the highest-scoring game (51-43) in the eighty-six-game series between these two southern rivals. It went on and on and on and on and on. Five overtimes! It was absolutely unbelievable.

The Tennessee Vols were nationally ranked and Alabama was not. The Tide had a number of chances to win the ball game, but in the end, it was a crushing loss. Bama just couldn't quite make the pivotal play. Couldn't make the big stop when necessary. Couldn't make the kick when necessary.

We were sitting in the booth saying to each other, "How—and when—is this thing going to end?" It sounds like a cop-out and very un-Alabama-like to say we almost won. But how could you get closer than this? What a fight.

There was plenty for coach Mike Shula and his team to be proud of during the 2003 game. Alabama ran ninety-nine offensive plays and made twenty-seven first downs. Junior placekicker Brian Bostick matched his career high with a forty-eight-yard field goal. Senior running back Shaud Williams became the tenth player in school history to rush for a thousand yards in a single season.

There were records and numbers flying all over the place. Unfortunately, the numbers that count, the ones that made up the final score, read: Tennessee 51, Alabama 43.

Close, but no cigar. Literally.

AH, CIGARS. BAMA COACHES, PLAYERS, AND FANS KNOW ALL TOO WELL what a cigar means on the third Saturday in October. It means victory for Alabama.

Like many of Alabama's great traditions, this one began early in the Bear Bryant era. In 1958, Bryant's first year as head coach at Alabama, the Vols beat Bama, 14-7. Then in '59, the game ended in a 7-7 tie.

Vols Coach Bowden Wyatt seemed at peace with the final score. "Nobody likes a tie," he told reporters after the game, "but it's better than getting beat."

I'm not so sure Coach Bryant concurred. The players who watched him kick down a locked locker room door after a 1965 tie with Tennessee would surely back up this statement. It's my guess he'd rather get beaten decisively than end up with a tie. We all know what he really wanted to do was win.

Tennessee once again got the best of the Tide in 1960, coming away with a 20-7 win. Then, finally, in the national-championship year of 1961, Coach Bryant got his fondest wish when Bama not only beat, but stomped Tennessee, 34-3, at Legion Field in Birmingham. Fullback Mike Fracchia set the tone by scoring the first touchdown on a make-it-look-easy, five-yard run. Quarterback Pat Trammel passed for one touchdown and later ran one yard for another. Halfback Billy Richardson scored as well.

After the game, Jim Goostree, Alabama's trainer from 1957 to 1984, handed out victory cigars. Somehow, this ritual that most people associate with weddings or births became a Bama tradition that coaches and players reserved solely for their Tennessee wins.

Photo courtesy of the Paul W. Bryant Museum, the University of Alabama.

Light 'em up!

Due to his twenty-seven years on the Bama sidelines, Goostree will always be known as an Alabama guy. But it just so happens that this man, so important to the Crimson and White, also happened to be a graduate of the University of Tennessee.

Sigmund Freud once famously said, "Sometimes a cigar is just a cigar." I doubt very much it was a Freudian thing. But there's no doubt the cigars they smoked after beating Tennessee meant a whole lot to Goostree and company.

Every player who knew Coach Bryant remembers his emphasis on the Tennessee game. He often said, "You found out what kind of person you were, player you were, and winner you were when you played against Tennessee."

Every Alabama player got his chance to find out what they were made of when it came time to face the Vols. Center Dwight Stephenson, a first-team all-American in 1979, remembers the Tennessee game his senior year.

"We had fallen behind, 17-0, going in at halftime," Stephenson said. "We were all a bit stunned, because I think we took them a little bit for granted. We went back in the locker room and Coach Bryant said, 'We are not going to go out there and do this thing the easy way; throw the football up and down the field and try to get lucky. We're going to do this thing the sure way and that's the hard way.' He said, 'We are going to run the football and our defense is going to stop them.'"

Damned if it didn't happen just the way the coach said it would.

"We scored twenty-four points," Stephenson continued. "And the defense never allowed them to score again in the game."

Stephenson never forgot that experience. He took the experience to heart and refers back to it often.

"Being part of that sort of thing still helps me in life," Stephenson said. "In business, things aren't easy. If they were, everybody would be doing it. It's a process. Just like that game."

The Tennessee game is always tough. It's almost always close. Linebacker Lee Roy Jordan, who played in the 1961 game (where postgame cigars were first enjoyed), said it was always a top priority to his team.

"Tennessee games were always tremendous," Jordan said. "Coach Bryant's theory was if you don't beat Tennessee, you don't have a good year or you certainly don't have a great year. That third week of October always pointed to the rest of the year for us."

Defense will win it for you.

More than a decade later, still looking to Coach Bryant for guidance, the 1973 team set the tone for the remainder of their season with their date with Tennessee. When the teams met at Legion Field in Birmingham, they were both highly ranked in the polls. They were also both undefeated.

Alabama wasted no time getting things started. On the first play after the kickoff, quarterback Gary Rutledge faked a handoff to the fullback. Both the Tennessee cornerback and safety charged to the line of scrimmage, leaving Bama wide receiver Wayne Wheeler wide open. Rutledge hit Wheeler with a perfect pass that he carried all the way to the end zone for six points.

A picture that speaks a thousand words.

"I couldn't believe both defenders bit on the fake," Rutledge said. "In that defense, the safety is like an extra linebacker, so you expected him to come up. But when the cornerback came, too, I knew if I could just get the ball to Wayne, we'd have a touchdown."

Right away, Bama took the lead. But this was Tennessee. The Vols fought hard and in the fourth quarter, the score was tied, 21-21. But Bama players

Robin Carey and Wilbur Jackson each then put up a touchdown. Bama took the day, 42-21.

Every win is satisfying. Especially against Tennessee. Not to take away from all the wins at Legion Field in Birmingham, or more recently at Bryant-Denny Stadium in Tuscaloosa. But there's nothing quite as sweet as beating the Vols at Neyland Stadium in Knoxville.

Bama star outside linebacker Cornelius Bennett concurs. In 1982, while he was still a high school student being recruited by colleges, he made a trip to Knoxville and watched Bama get beaten by the Vols.

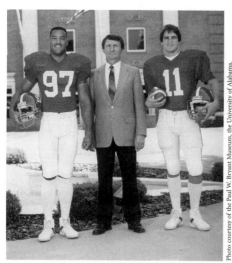

Cornelius Bennett, Coach Ray Perkins and quarterback (and current head coach) Mike Shula.

"I already knew I was going to Alabama," said Bennett. "But I made the trip and Tennessee won. I remember being in the Tennessee locker room. They were passing out cigars and throwing oranges at the Alabama players walking off the field. That just stuck with me."

Then Bennett came to Alabama as a player. In his first three years, the Vols beat his team. Then his senior year, 1986, Bennett and his bunch, led by Coach Ray Perkins, made one last trip to Knoxville.

"I think everybody that played that day probably had the best game of their careers," Bennett said. "Offense just ran over them. On defense, I made every play that a linebacker could make. Just to walk out of that stadium on the opposite side of it and remember that '82 game, it was a great feeling."

Bama won big, by the way, 56-28, and also began a nine-year unbeaten streak against the Vols.

Center Wes Neighbors, Bennett's teammate, said the 1986 Tennessee game is his greatest memory as a player.

"They came out with these orange shoes," Neighbors said. "And we just went out there and ran the same play forty-eight times! I think we had three

Defensive end Antwan Odom (#98) sacks Tennessee quarterback Casey Clausen (#7).

backs over two hundred yards. One time we lined up and we had run the sweep so many times, we look out and there is nobody in front of us. Everybody was on the right. I think actually my roommate, Bill Collins, checked off. He looked up at Shula and said, 'We can't go there.' But we ran up the middle for a touchdown. It was great."

The one visit to Neyland Stadium I will never forget as a broadcaster was in 1990. This was Gene Stallings's first year as coach. Bama was a huge underdog going in, having lost its first three games that year and counting its only wins against two less-than-impressive opponents, Vanderbilt and Southwestern Louisiana. Tennessee on the other hand, was ranked No. 3 in the nation.

Shaud Williams in for a touchdown.

181

The game was all about the kickers. Field goals had produced all the points on the board. Late in the game, the score was tied, 6-6. Tennessee attempted a field goal, but the kick was blocked by the Tide's Stacy Harrison. Bama got the ball at the Tennessee thirty-seven yard line. They ran three plays to little avail. Now it was time for Philip Doyle to attempt yet another kick—this one would have to sail forty-seven yards through the uprights. And sail it did.

"At first I thought the kick was blocked," Doyle said. "But the ball had felt right when it left my foot."

Sometimes it's good to be the kicker. Bama won, 9-6. The team hoisted Doyle onto their collective shoulders and the visiting Bama fans went nuts. That was sweet. But sweeter still was the silence coming from the remaining one hundred thousand orange-clad fans. In a stadium so well known for its noise that Bama, to this day, practices the week before the ballgame with crowd noise blaring through the loudspeakers so they won't be rattled come game day; there's nothing quite like making one hundred thousand people hush up.

Quarterback Jay Barker and Coach Gene Stallings after the 1992 win over Tennessee.

WHAT IS IT ABOUT THE TENNESSEE RIVALRY THAT GETS PLAYERS AND coaches so incredibly riled up? Legendary Bama Coach Frank Thomas was said to have gotten so nervous before the Tennessee game that he put the lit end of his cigar in his mouth. (Again, with the cigars.)

The late, great Coach Ken Donahue, who as a former Tennessee player and coach as well as a longtime Alabama assistant coach (1964-1984), was perhaps one of the best qualified to speak to this rivalry which currently has Alabama ahead by a nose (43-36-7).

"The game has always served as a measuring stick for both teams," Donahue said. "I played for General Bob Neyland at Tennessee. He talked about how the test would come against Alabama. I worked under Coach Paul "Bear" Bryant at Alabama. He talked about how we never would know what kind of team we had until we played Tennessee."

So, there's a lot of pride. A lot of respect. But I still say there's too much damn orange.

SEVENTEEN

The Bear Dies

Whatever It Was,
He Had a Lot of It

ON JANUARY 26, 1983, I HAD JUST FLOWN INTO BIRMINGHAM FROM Salt Lake City, after broadcasting a hockey game. Upon landing at the Birmingham airport, I went straight to my office at WERC Radio, where I was doing an afternoon sports talk show. I picked up my mail, which had

Photo courtesy of the Paul W. Bryant Museum, the University of Alabama.

accumulated during my road trip, and was heading to my desk when I stopped cold in my tracks. Somebody in the newsroom was yelling, "Coach Bryant just passed away!"

It was hard to believe. A chill went down my spine as I remembered what the coach had said a year or so back when a reporter asked him whether he planned to retire. "Quit?" Bryant had answered. "No way. I'd croak in a week."

Bryant had just retired as head coach a month before. And now, at age sixty-nine, he was gone. It was just unbelievable.

The guys in the newsroom confirmed the sad news. Immediately, I went into the studio and got to work. I broke into the regularly scheduled programming with a bulletin and then didn't leave the airwaves until hours and hours later. We just opened the phones and let people call in and talk about what Coach Bryant meant to them. There was story after story from regular folks who considered themselves lucky to have met him just once. "He shook my hand in 1965," or "He took time out of his day to say hello to me."

We talked to a lot of ordinary, everyday fans. But we also got every important person you can think of to talk to us on the air. You name them! They were on! Our producers lined up college coaches, baseball people, sports executives, everybody! They all had a Bear Bryant story. Kids who played

Photo courtesy of the Paul W. Bryant Museum, the University of Alabama.

for him. Kids recruited by him. Mammas and daddies would say, "I remember that day he recruited little Billy. He came to the house, and it was like the Lord himself had walked through the door." Or "I was driving down the interstate once, and there he was in the car next to me. I couldn't believe it!" Some were the smallest of remembrances.

It's amazing that so many callers got through because, as Clem Gryska, remembers, the phone lines were jammed all over the city. "You couldn't make a call from here to there," Gryska said.

One way or another, everyone in Alabama quickly heard the news. We stayed on the air from just after noon until I'm not sure when. It had long since turned dark outside. It was probably going on midnight. Everyone at WERC was pitching in. I'm sure I took a "potty break" in there somewhere, but I'll be darned if I can remember when. It was nonstop "Coach Bryant talk" all day and all night.

People were in shock that day. Especially his close friends. Bryant's longtime radio producer, Bert Bank, went to the hospital to see him the day he died.

Photo courtesy of the Paul W. Bryant Museum, the University of Alabama.

"I heard early in the morning that he had a heart attack," Bank said. "So I went by the drugstore and bought a magazine called *What I Know About Football.* When you opened it up, the pages were blank! I went to the hospital to give it to him but they were working on him in the room, so I didn't go in. By the time I got back to my office, I got the call that he had died."

Coach Gryska saw Bryant the day he went into the hospital. "It was off-season and I was in my office. It was kind of a nice afternoon for January. Coach Bryant popped his head in and says, 'I think I'll go walk a little bit.' He came back afterwards and said, 'I feel pretty good.' Then by 6:30 they had taken him to the hospital due to a heart attack. The next morning Coach Sam Bailey came to the office and told us everything was fine—he was up and eating breakfast. Later, we were at Bryant Hall having lunch when his secretary called and said, 'You better get to the hospital right away.' The hospital was only two minutes away, but by the time we got there he was gone."

Everyone was in shock. Even though his close friends knew he had been hiding that fact that he was ill for some time, it was still a shock. He had been in and out of the hospital several times over the last couple of years but no one thought it was possible to lose Paul Bryant.

Coach Bryant's funeral procession moves slowly past Bryant-Denny stadium.

On the day of the funeral, WERC did live radio coverage. We had a reporter, Tony Giles, who is now the public address announcer for Alabama football and basketball, at the grave site. I anchored the coverage from outside Elmwood Cemetery, setting the scene and talking to the scores of luminaries and politicians who walked by on their way to pay their respects.

Mourners were lined up along the highway all the way from Tuscaloosa to Birmingham to watch the funeral procession pass by.

Coach Gryska remembers the procession vividly. "It began in Tuscaloosa," he said. "And when we went by the stadium, well, that was a tear-jerker there. That's where we played and did all the work. It was a very sad day."

Jeremiah Castille, a Bama defensive back from 1979 to 1982, remembers being overwhelmed by the outpouring of grief.

"For sixty miles people are lined up along the highway crying," Castille said. "They were just bawling their eyes out on the overpass! I said, man, this is bigger than I ever imagined."

Some ten thousand people jammed outside the church in

Fans line the interstate overpasses waiting for the motorcade to pass.

Birmingham to listen to the service on the loudspeakers. Everyone else around the state watched the funeral on TV or listened on the radio. There was live coverage all day long.

The whole thing—the funeral, the emotion, the massive amounts of media attention—was absolutely incredible to me. Where else would the death of a football coach get nonstop, statewide coverage? Truly, the only things I can compare this event to are President Kennedy's funeral and the recent coverage of the funeral of Pope John Paul II.

The state of Alabama ground to a halt. What I found impressive is that on this day, it didn't matter whether you were an Auburn fan or a Bama fan that day. Everyone mourned Coach Bryant.

Photo courtesy of the the *Birmingham News*

Buses carrying Bama players and staff arrive at Birmingham's Elmwood Cemetery for Coach Bryant's service.

As of 1983 I had lived in Alabama for only five years. From the moment I came to town, I knew Coach Bryant was important. But looking back, I don't think I truly understood what he meant to people until the day he died.

What a life he lived. Many Alabama fans can recite his incredible story by heart. He was born Paul William Bryant in tiny Fordyce, Arkansas (population three thousand), in 1913. Technically, he was born in the even tinier burg of Moro Bottom, which was really just a chunk of land with six family farms, including the Bryants' 260 acres, where they raised cotton and vegetables.

Bryant was the eleventh of twelve children. Three of his siblings died. By all accounts, it was a hardscrabble life not uncommon to many Americans during this era. The Bryants were poor—Paul was thirteen when he got his first pair of shoes. There is an oft-told story of the town's children teasing young Paul when he rode into town with his mother to sell vegetables from a wagon pulled by a mule.

Bryant never romanticized these depression-era stories—it was always his intention to escape his hometown and never return to that kind of humiliating poverty. But he did believe that adversity made you a better, stronger person. He drew from this in later life.

Another oft-told story is how fourteen-year-old Paul Bryant got his nickname "Bear."

"A carnival came through town and they had this scraggly bear," Bryant once told reporters. "A man was offering anybody a dollar a minute to wrestle it. Somebody dared me to do it. I said I would."

Bryant got in the ring with the bear, who was less-than-impressive for his species, but a bear nonetheless! Paul charged the bear and tried to pin him down. He was holding the animal in a headlock, trying to keep it from rolling on top of him when the circus man, wanting more excitement for the crowd whispered, "Let him up!"

The bear's muzzle came off and he bit Paul in the ear. The boy ran out of the theater. When he came back to collect his money, the man was gone. All Paul got was a scar, a story, and a nickname that would last the rest of his life.

Young Bear Bryant played football from the eighth grade on, despite the fact that his parents belonged to the Church of God and didn't smoke, drink, go to the movies, or attend football games . . . even his.

As the stories go, Bear was a good player (he was all-state for the Fordyce Fighting Redbugs his sophomore year), but he got into a lot of fights. Pardon the pop psychology, but maybe this is why he was such a disciplinarian when he became a head coach. It was a "Do as I say, not as I did" kind of thing.

His senior year in high school, when he was six-foot-three and 190 pounds, Alabama assistant coach Hank Crisp recruited him to play football for the Crimson Tide. He was not quite prepared for college academically, so he spent his first year in Tuscaloosa taking high school classes in Spanish and math. After that, he enrolled at the university and he was on his way.

After graduation, Bryant married his sweetheart, Mary Harmon Black, and elected to stay on at Alabama to work as an assistant under coach Frank Thomas. He stayed four years, then in the spring of 1940, went to Vanderbilt to work for Coach Red Sanders. The next year, he interviewed for a position as head coach at Arkansas, but World War II got in the way. When the Japanese bombed Pearl Harbor, Bryant joined the navy.

Navy man Paul Bryant.

During his commission, Bryant's troop ship was reportedly rammed and dead in the water for three days. Some two hundred sailors were lost at sea. Bryant, of course, survived. It's funny, but this amazing tale is virtually unknown around Alabama. People always want to talk about football. The war was merely a blip on the way to becoming a gridiron hero and legend.

After the war, Bryant ran into Redskins owner George Preston Marshall, whom he met while he was still working for Coach Thomas. Marshall offered him an assistant coaching job, but Bryant knew he wanted to be a head coach. So when Marshall recommended him for a job at the University of Maryland, Bryant headed northeast immediately.

Bryant won his first game at Maryland, 60-6. Not a bad start. He left after one year, though (he finished 6-2-1), to accept the head coaching position at Kentucky. During his eight years at Kentucky, Bryant piled up a winning record of sixty wins, twenty-three losses, and five ties. This was an incredible accomplishment at a school not exactly known for football. Basketball was always king at Kentucky. In fact, it has been said that part of the reason for Bryant's departure from Kentucky was the fact that he felt football would never be the school's first priority as long as the legendary Adolph Rupp coached the basketball team. (Interesting note: both Rupp and Bryant went on to become the winningest coaches in their respective sports.)

In 1954 Bryant took over as head coach at Texas A&M. His first year, a rebuilding period for the struggling program, was also the year of the famous "Junction Boys." They were so named because of Bryant's intense, off-campus, rough-and-tumble, pre-season camp held in the dusty town of Junction. When Coach Gene Stallings, who had been one of Bryant's Junction Boys, was asked if the camp was really as tough as they say he answered, "All I know is, we went out there in two buses and came back in one."

After piling up three winning seasons at Texas A&M, Bryant made a move that surprised perhaps everyone but himself, when he returned to Alabama in 1958 as head coach saying that "Mama called."

In his twenty-five years at Alabama, Coach Bryant chalked up nothing but winning seasons. He nailed down six national championships, thirteen SEC titles, and took his team to twenty-four consecutive bowl games. In 1981, a year before he retired, Bryant became the winningest coach of all time when Alabama beat Auburn for his 315th victory.

Dozens of books have been written about this incredible man. Movies have been made about him. (I've always envisioned John Wayne in the part.) He still has a strong and constant presence in Tuscaloosa—there is the Bryant Museum, the Bryant Conference Center, Bryant Drive, Bryant Hall, and, of course, Bryant-Denny Stadium.

Why do we remember him so well and so fondly? It has to be the winning. No question, if Coach Bryant won only now and again, we wouldn't be having this discussion. But to hear his former players tell it, the way he went about winning was just as important as the final score. Beyond that, the incredible status he achieved was about so much more than winning. It was as if he was a de facto college football commissioner while running his own team at the same time. He was a distinguished, imposing figure with an undeniable aura about him. He had a way of walking—a slow amble—and a way of talking—a low growl—that cemented his mystique.

Legendary Alabama lineman Bob Baumhower, who would later star for the Miami Dolphins and then become a successful restaurateur, credits Coach Bryant with all his triumphs.

"I had a great first year at Alabama, then I slacked off some," Baumhower said. "I lost my starting position and was going to quit. Well, Coach Bryant called me in his office. He said, 'I don't like talking to quitters, but since you're here, sit your butt down.' He explained to me why I didn't deserve to be a starter. By the end of the meeting, I begged for a chance to come back. He gave me a second chance. Today, every success I have, every win that I have, in my opinion, came from the fact that Coach Bryant cared enough to talk to me and turn the light on for me."

Alabama athletic director Mal Moore, a player and coach under Bryant, sums it up this way: "He's a name that will be and should be remembered,"

Moore said. "He was a great, great ambassador for the university and for the state of Alabama. He had something about him that attracted people to him. To quote Bobby Marks, whatever he had or whatever it was, he had a lot of it."

According to Moore, it was Bryant's talent as a motivator that made him such a winner and ultimately, so beloved: "Coach Bryant used to say that man to man, his teams weren't as good—or worth a damn is what he said—but they didn't know it. They believed they were good and they believed in him. So he put them through the test. He worked them. It was a oneness that was unbelievable."

Coach Bryant was respected. Some say he was feared. But one word that keeps cropping up when his former players speak of him, as unlikely as this may sound, is *love*.

"I loved him," former Bama linebacker Barry Krauss said. "The biggest thrill to me was that I could walk in and talk to him and that he knew me and cared about me."

Jack Rutledge, who played and coached under Bryant, identifies the nuance of when the love kicked in.

"Coach Bryant would never get close to his players while they were playing for him," Rutledge said. "When you were working for him or you were under his supervision, he was strictly business. But as soon as you graduated or as soon as you left, then he became your best friend."

Most, if not all of the Bama players who went on to play in the NFL, cite Coach Bryant as the single biggest influence on their lives. I remember Joe Namath doing an interview after the Jets won the Super Bowl in 1969, when he said, "As Coach Bryant used to say . . ."

Late in the 2004 season, I saw at a Jets game former Alabama defensive tackle Marty Lyons, who played for the New York Jets and now does their radio broadcasts. He had a group of media guys completely engrossed as he told one Coach Bryant story after another. Incredible. Coach Bryant has been gone more than twenty years, and they're still talking about him on game day.

Alabama linebacker Lee Roy Jordan, later a Dallas Cowboy superstar, is often asked to compare Coach Bryant to his other legendary coach, Tom Landry.

"Coach Landry was a brilliant guy," Jordan said. "But he was not near the motivator or the guy who could excite you about playing the game. He felt like you were a professional. You were paid so you should do your job. But Coach Bryant is still the one I remember most. Just the way he taught us and motivated and conditioned us into believing that we could win at any point in the game.

"Against Georgia Tech we were down, 15-0, at half time. We went back and beat them, 16-15. He had a knack for what to do and when to motivate us. Sometimes it was shout and scream and yell. Sometimes it was nothing. He knew how to read the team and what they needed. I had fourteen years with Coach Landry, and it was terrific. But the four years with Coach Bryant overshadows it."

Photo courtesy of the Paul W. Bryant Museum, the University of Alabama.

"I played with Lee Roy during that Georgia game," Jack Rutledge said. "And I remember before the Tennessee game that year, Coach Bryant said, 'Today we become one. If you don't feel that way, you don't belong here. When Steve runs, we run. When John blocks, we block. Now remember this, the game is over, you come back in the shower, you walk by the mirror, and only you and the man in the mirror knows if you did the best you could. You walk out of the dressing room, you see your girlfriend, you hug your mama, and you reach out, you touch your daddy's hand. And only you and the man knows if you did the best you could.'"

Well said.

Coach Bryant was a legend—an incredible, colorful, quotable character. There is no doubt he set big goals and worked incessantly to meet them. He touched the lives of scores of players by practicing his brand of tough love consistently and fairly. We remember Coach Bryant so well because he was a winner. And we miss him so much because of how he won.

They just don't make 'em like that anymore.

The Gene Stallings Era

The Second Coming

ALABAMA FANS GOT SOME GREAT NEWS IN 1990: GENE STALLINGS was on his way "home" to Alabama to become the new head football coach. And he was coming not a minute too soon.

After Bear Bryant retired in 1982, and sadly, passed away in 1983, Bama football had spent the rest of that decade weathering some serious ups and downs.

Coach Gene Stallings.

Coach Ray Perkins came in 1983 and stayed for four seasons, three of them winning ones. Then, Bill Curry took over in 1987, and despite three winning—if not perfect—seasons, left at the end of 1989 to take the head coaching job at Kentucky.

Then in 1990 it was announced that Stallings was the man. He was all too familiar with the pressure and incredibly high, national championship level of expectation that fans of the Crimson Tide had for their coach. True to form, it didn't seem to faze the straight talking Stallings a bit.

"The expectation level is high at the

University of Alabama, and it should be," Stallings said. "What's wrong with people expecting excellence?"

Gene "Bebes" Stallings could not have had a better résumé for this job. Born in Paris, Texas, in 1935, Stallings attended Paris High School and excelled in football and baseball, taking all-district honors in both sports. He went to college at Texas A&M, where he got a degree in physical education and played football. Stallings has the incredible distinction of being one of Bear Bryant's "Junction Boys," the 1954 team that Bryant took off campus and put through a grueling pre-season boot camp in his first year as A&M's head coach.

Stallings was one of just thirty-five players who returned on that single bus from the grueling Junction experience. He played two more seasons under Bryant. His senior year he was an all-Southwest Conference end and was named cocaptain of the undefeated (9-0-1) team.

Photo courtesy of the *Birmingham News*

Coach Bryant gives the victorious Gene Stallings a lift after the Aggies beat the Tide 20-16 in the 1968 Cotton Bowl.

After graduation, Stallings stayed on at A&M as an assistant coach. He evidently kept scrupulous notes on Bryant's teachings, which helped tremendously when he later collaborated with him on a book about football techniques, *Bear Bryant on Winning Football.*

When Bryant was offered the top job at Alabama in 1957, he brought Stallings along with him. He was defensive coordinator on the national championship teams of 1961 and 1964.

Then, in 1965, when he was just twenty-nine years old, Texas A&M asked him to come back as head coach and athletic director. Stallings said yes.

After he heard the news that Stallings would be following in his footsteps and taking the A&M job, Coach Bryant gave an interview to the *Houston Post*:

It's the first time I've cried in twenty or thirty years," Bryant said. "And believe me, I really did. I cried because I'm so proud that one of my little Junction Boys is going back there to take over. And secondly, I cried because I'm so upset about losing him. Shoot, with Stallings gone, I may have to go back to work. A&M could go back to Rockne, and they could not have picked a better man. He will be the best football coach the school ever had and that includes father.

("Father" was Bryant's way of referring to himself. He was no doubt teasing his young protégé.)

In his book *The Legend of Bear Bryant*, Mickey Herskowitz tells a great story about this moment in college football history. A writer named Bob Curran told Herskowitz that he had walked into Bryant's hotel room during the above mentioned interview, which was taking place by phone. He said he thought Bryant indeed looked quite choked up and asked a friend in the room, "What's wrong with Paul?"

"He just lost an assistant coach," the man whispered.

All business on the sidelines.

"How old was he?" Curran asked.

"Twenty-nine."

"My God!" exclaimed Curran, "That's awfully young. How did he die?"

"Oh, he didn't die," the friend assured him. "He just went to Texas A&M."

The Aggies struggled during Stallings first couple of years. Then in 1967, after losing their first four games, the team turned it around and finished the season with six straight wins, their conference title, and an invitation to the Cotton Bowl.

Their postseason opponent—The University of Alabama.

The week before the big game, the teams' coaches had a ball playfully baiting each other in the press. When Stallings arrived for a press conference wearing muddy boots and an old dirty cap, Bryant ribbed him: "I refuse to have my picture taken with someone who looks like that." Stallings (who later returned in a tuxedo!) shot back, "You taught me to work. I can party after the game."

Stallings had every reason to party when his Aggies beat Bama, 20-16. By all accounts, Bryant was fairly good-natured about the loss, showing all the good sportsmanship he could muster by helping to carry Stallings to the locker room.

In 1972 Stallings was fired from Texas A&M. A small blemish on a near-perfect résumé. He bounced back immediately when fellow-Texan Tom Landry hired him as an assistant coach for the Dallas Cowboys. Stallings stayed in Dallas an incredible fourteen years and during that time, the Cowboys put up some incredible numbers. They won seven division titles (1973, 1976-79, 1981, and 1985), three conference championships (1975, 1977, and 1978) and played in three Super Bowls (1976, 1978, and 1979). They were Super Bowl champs in 1978.

After his amazing run in Dallas, in 1986 Stallings was hired for his first NFL head coaching job when he took over the St. Louis Cardinals who then moved to Arizona in 1988. Working for the Bidwell family, who owned the Cardinals, was from all reports a trying experience. According to print reports in both St.

Photo courtesy of Kent Gidley, the University of Alabama.

Setting the stage for another national title.

Louis and Arizona, the fans were understanding of the Cardinals' shortcomings. In fact, Stallings became a beloved personality in both Missouri and Arizona. The same could not be said for the team's ownership group. Many people to this day feel that Stallings was let go from the Cardinals not because of the won/loss record but indeed because the fans liked him, which really annoyed the owners. Then in 1990, Stallings came "home" to Bama.

Granted, things did start slowly. Bama lost its first three, including a 17-16 nail-biter to Georgia. They appeared to turn things around though, with back-to-back wins over Vanderbilt and Southwest

Louisiana. Then Bama traveled to Knoxville to face third-ranked rival Tennessee.

Bama held the Vols to just two field goals then won it, 9-6, with a thrilling, last-minute forty-seven-yard Philip Doyle kick. Faith was renewed! After an especially meaningful (16-7) win over Auburn, the Tide lost to Browning Nagle and the Louisville Cardinals in the Fiesta Bowl and finished the season 7-5.

The Tide truly turned in 1991, but it took a humiliating (35-0) loss to Florida to get things started. After enduring that beating in the Swamp, Bama didn't lose another game all year. In fact, the Crimson Tide would go on to win their next twenty-eight games in a row!

For most schools, an 11-1 season would be stunning. Winning twenty-

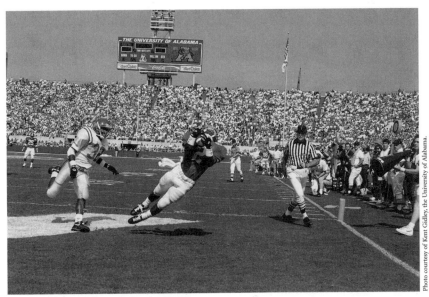

"The Deuce," David Palmer, scores against Ole Miss.

Photo courtesy of Kent Gidley, the University of Alabama.

eight games in a row and going 30-0-1 in one stretch would be outrageous. But remember, this is Alabama, a university where winning championships is as expected as the sun coming up in the morning. So, nothing would be right with the Alabama world until they brought home a national championship. And that would happen in the incredible year of 1992.

When Coach Stallings came to Tuscaloosa, his tremendous reputation preceded him. People were very reverent, some going so far as to say this was the second coming of Bear Bryant. There was no denying that Stallings and Bryant, both solid, trustworthy, honest, tough, plain-spoken men, were cut from the same piece of cloth. Right away, I saw that Stallings had that Bear-like demeanor that could be businesslike and almost gruff, but ultimately fair and respectful.

Every week, as I do now, I would conduct a pregame interview with the coach. One particular time, I don't remember the exact date, I went out to practice a few days before our interview. Both the Alabama centers were hurt that week. So Coach Stallings had Patrick Hape, a tight end who still plays for the Denver Broncos, snapping the football. He needed to know that some one could fill in if push came to shove on Saturday.

So, later we were taping the pregame show and I said, "Coach, I've got to ask you about Patrick Hape and the experiment of him snapping the football. How'd that work out?"

He looked at my tape recorder and said, "Turn that dang thing off!"

I said, "Excuse me?"

I've seen that look.

Photo courtesy of Kent Gidley, the University of Alabama.

He said, "Turn off that machine!"

He then asked me if I ever heard him publicly talking about Hape taking snaps. I said no, but I was there. I saw it. And it was in the newspapers.

He asked me again, "But did you ever hear me talk about it?"

I said no.

"So," he said, "We're not going to talk about it. Now, start that machine back up!"

Well, I saw the boy taking snaps. I figured it was public domain. But in my line of work, the last thing you want to do is tick off the coach . . . especially one who's going to be around for a while. So, we wrapped it up and I told him good luck.

He said, "Eli, thank you very much. You are a classy professional. I've enjoyed working with you, and I look forward to talking with you after the ball game."

The coach and I on the practice field in Tampa Florida, prior to the 1997 Outback Bowl against Michigan. This was the coach's final game at Alabama.

So, he gave me a bit of a verbal spanking for asking a question he didn't want asked. The fans at home had no idea because we edited it out. He made sure he got his message across to me, but then he let me know he wasn't mad at me. His last words were to make sure I didn't leave with my chin down around my ankles.

He knew how to handle people, whether they were media guys, his staff, or his players. Especially when it came to players, he knew how to bring out the best in people. He knew when to be tough or when someone needed to be built back up.

Quarterback Jay Barker, who played for Stallings from 1991 to 1994, was a great example of this. Coach Stallings saw that even though Jay might not have been able to throw the ball eighty yards in the air or that he wasn't the fastest man on the planet, this guy was a winner.

"I couldn't throw a spiral my first week," Barker laughed. "I don't know if I ever threw a spiral by some people's idea the whole time I was at Alabama!"

Well, he managed to throw a few during an especially memorable game against the Georgia Bulldogs in 1994. Barker and Georgia quarterback Eric Zeier were two of the top quarterbacks in all of America that year, and now they were going head to head.

"The week before," Barker said, "the coaches told me that Eric was going to throw for three hundred yards, you're going to maybe throw for a hundred. I said, 'Look, as long as we win the game.'"

Indeed, Zeier came out throwing, while on the other side of the field, Barker got benched.

"I was struggling," Barker remembered. "So Coach Stallings said, 'You need to sit over here and watch. You need to get your act together and see things clearly.'"

National Championship winning quarterback Jay Barker.

Photo courtesy of Kent Gidley, the University of Alabama.

Well, things cleared up for Barker. He went back in and defenders were all over him like a cheap suit, but he would not go down. He refused to be tackled. By the fourth quarter, he had already thrown for over three hundred yards. Then, when everything was hanging in the balance, he hit Toderick Malone for a twenty-yard pass and he ran it the rest of the way for a touchdown. Bama won it, 29-28.

"That game did a lot for my own confidence," Barker said. "It allowed me to show what I could do. In the past, our defense was so great that we played very conservatively on offense."

The normally conservative Barker ended up throwing an incredible 396 yards that night! He was personally thrilled that the game was on ESPN, and he was able to share his Christian faith with the audience during a postgame interview. He was also extremely grateful to Coach Stallings for sitting him down early in the game.

"Coach Stallings was tough," Barker said. "But he was such a motivator."

Stallings motivated his players in many different ways. Some of his former players enjoy giving him a hard time when they remember some of his motivational techniques . . . his special Friday night movies, for instance.

"Coach Stallings, he always believed in his movies!" cornerback Antonio Langham said. "You had to go to the movies on Friday night. But it wasn't our movie. It was his movie. He picked it. And it always had something to do with guys fighting in the military. I think we went to see *A Few Good Men* once."

Barker says they weren't all military movies. "We saw *Home Alone* before the Auburn game. We were all like, what's he going to get out of this one?

Then he says, 'Look at all the obstacles this kid faced! You have to have strategy. You have to have a plan!'"

"My senior year, he let the captains pick the movie," fullback Kevin Turner said. "I picked one that was so bad; I think it was *Highlander II*."

"Yeah," center Roger Shultz said, "We picked *Goodfellas* one time. It had all that cussing in it. We loved it. He said, 'That's awful. You beat the guy up and put him in the trunk. What's the lesson in that?'"

So, Coach Stallings went back to selecting the movie. And motivating his team. The 1992 season was all about motivation. And goals. From the start of spring practice in 1992, Stallings, his staff, and his team had one goal: to win the national championship.

Photo courtesy of Kent Gidley, the University of Alabama.

Coach Stallings with his successor, Mike DuBose in the background.

"I didn't really know we were going to do it until we were 9-0," Stallings said. "Then I knew."

The crowning achievement for Stallings and his team that year was their Sugar Bowl victory, which nailed down the title for the Tide. As Bama quietly made their way down to New Orleans, the players found themselves contrasting in every way with the flamboyant, trash-talking Miami players. Stallings just focused and kept his players on track.

"We went down to New Orleans and tried to keep things as regular as possible," Stallings said. "There was all this hoopla with the bowl, and we participated in the things that we were supposed to. But as far as practice, we tried to keep things normal and go through it like it was a regular week."

With all the temptations of bowl-hosting New Orleans, keeping things normal was perhaps the biggest accomplishment of all. Especially when the coach elected to keep his team in town the night before the game.

"I took some criticism in the press for keeping the team in New Orleans," Stallings remembered. "Miami had moved their team out. But I thought it was more of a distraction to move. I brought the whole team, and I'm most proud of the fact that no one missed curfew. Not one player. I mean, you could take one hundred preachers to New Orleans and one of them would slip out. On our team, no one did."

The 1992 championship was the highlight of Coach Stallings's incredible career as Alabama head coach, in which he led his teams to a record of 70-16-1.

In 1996 Stallings retired as head coach and moved back to Paris, Texas, with his wife, Ruth Anne, and his son, John Mark, who was diagnosed with Down syndrome as a child and is now in his early forties.

Folks in Tuscaloosa got to know Johnny well over the years. He was a welcome presence on the sidelines and at team events. He still is an enthusiastic Bama fan. During his time as head coach, Stallings was incredibly active doing charity work with disabled children. It seemed he just couldn't do enough for these kids. He even wrote a book called *Another Season* about the experience of raising a handicapped child.

Photo courtesy of Kent Gidley, the University of Alabama.

This might be my favorite picture of Coach Stallings. His love for his son, John Mark, knows no bounds.

Coach Stallings currently serves on the President's Commission on Intellectual Disabilities. The Rise Program on the University of Alabama campus recently dedicated the John Mark Stallings Playground in Johnny's name. Ultimately, Gene Stallings, who also has four daughters, Anna Lee, Laurie, Jackie, and Martha Kate, is perhaps as well known and beloved for his title of "father" as he is for his title of "head coach."

When you stop and reflect on the great Gene Stallings story, from Junction Boy to Texas A&M coach to national championship-winning Alabama coach, the comparisons to Bear Bryant's own larger-than-life tale are inevitable. Even legendary Dallas Cowboys coach Tom Landry, Stallings's former boss, made this connection:

Stallings worked for Bear Bryant, played for Bear Bryant, and he is a lot like Bear Bryant. He's a good solid, fundamental coach," Landry said. "He knows the game very well, teaches it well, and expects nothing but the best from the people he coaches. If I were the parent of an eighteen-year-old son, he'd be the type of person for whom I would want my son to play.

"Coach Bryant was a guy that I grew up wanting to play for," Jay Barker said. "I feel like in Gene Stallings, I got the next best thing."

Stallings has heard himself compared to Bryant many times over the years. But typically, he modestly waves away the comparisons.

"There's just one Coach Bryant," Stallings said. "He set the bar, and the rest of us are just trying to do the best we can. I was always fond of saying, 'People in Alabama loved Coach Bryant. They just tolerated the rest of us.'"

Both Bryant and Stallings were straightforward, dedicated men who demanded excellence from those around them. They had great, great football minds and knew how to handle people. They both were winners.

But is it possible that in his six years as head coach of Alabama, Gene Stallings left behind something even more meaningful and magical than all those wins of the twenty-five-year Bear Bryant era? It just might be. Because when he came back and built a winning team he showed us it could be done again, post-Bear. He left us with hope. And that may be the greatest gift of all.

NINETEEN

The 1992 Championship

But We Haven't Won Anything Yet

IN 1990 GENE STALLINGS TOOK THE HELM AS ALABAMA'S HEAD coach. That first year, the team finished with a respectable if not laudatory 7-5 record after opening 0-3. The 1991 season was better: Bama won eleven and lost one. Then came 1992. It was a good year for Alabama fans. A very good year.

National Title #12 is on the horizon.

Photo courtesy of Kent Gidley, the University of Alabama.

It happened quietly and matter-of-factly. In 1992 Bama simply chalked up one win after another.

Oddly enough, though, all this winning didn't necessarily inspire the expected accolades from all circles. For some people, the winning just wasn't enough. Everywhere you looked—the newspaper, TV, and radio— there were nay-saying journalists. After every Bama win, ESPN's Lee Corso would say, "They're the worst 3-0 football team I've ever seen." Then the next week you'd hear him again: "They're the worst 4-0 team I've seen." Then weeks later, "They're the worst 8-0 team," and finally, "I know they're 10-0, but I just don't get it."

I mean, come on. Was Bama looking like Rodney Dangerfield? No respect.

Even for Coach Stallings, the winning wasn't enough. When the record was 3-0 he would say, "Don't let's get ahead of ourselves. We haven't won anything yet." I remember telling the coach one day, "Coach, don't worry. It's only Louisiana Tech coming in on Saturday!" Yikes! (What was I thinking?) It was like I had insulted the Stallings family name. He said sternly, but respectfully, "You don't think this game is big? Just go out and lose it and then see how big it was." Good point.

Soon, the team was 4-0. Again, the coach's comment: "We still haven't won anything." Even after finding his team at 11-0 he said, "Hold on. We haven't gotten what we want."

Coach Stallings was by no means downplaying his team's accomplishments. On the contrary, he was beaming with pride for a team that delivered the winningest season since Coach Bryant had left the university. But Stallings had his eye on the prize: the national championship. That was the goal. Not to go 11-0 or 12-0. The goal was to win the championship, however you got there.

"We talked about the national championship all the time," quarterback Jay Barker remembered. "We broke it down how we were going to do it in summer practice. That was our goal. To bring it back to Alabama."

Until the goal was achieved, Stallings and company just couldn't rest. So this Energizer Bunny of a team kept going and going and going.

Nineteen ninety-two was an unusual year in another way. There was a new system in place whereby Bama, as the SEC's Western Division champs (at 11-0) had to play Florida, the Eastern Division champs (at 8-3), in the first-ever Southeastern Conference Championship game. The NCAA rules allowed conferences of twelve or more teams to hold a championship game. Since the SEC had picked up Arkansas and South Carolina that year, they were now a twelve-team conference that would be split into two six-team divisions.

THE ATTRACTION OF A CHAMPIONSHIP GAME IS LARGELY FINANCIAL. Here's an opportunity to pack an eighty-thousand-seat stadium and bring in beaucoup TV dollars. Personally, I loved it because a championship game meant I got to do what I love to do: broadcast another game. But for Bama, it was an additional step that could have tripped them up on their way to their goal.

In years past, at this point in the season, Bama (having won eleven games) would have been readying themselves to play Miami on New Year's Day for the national championship. But this year, they had to get by the Gators first. As it turned out, the game was not an easy one. It was the quintessential nail-biter.

Even though Florida was a ten-point underdog coming into the game, they managed to tie the score with only 3:39 left to play. Florida had the ball, and their quarterback Shane Matthews called a short pass play. Alabama was in its zone defense. Cornerback Antonio Langham gambled that the hitch, a six- or seven-yard route the Gators had run earlier, courtesy of receiver Monty Duncan, was coming again. Langham actually positioned himself behind the receiver so Matthews couldn't see him. He was hiding back there!

Matthews did indeed throw a hitch route pass, intended again for Duncan, but Langham leapt up, snagged the ball from the receiver, and ran it back for a thrilling touchdown. The extra point was good (Bama won, 28-21) and its SEC title was a done deal.

Coach Stallings's comment? "This is nice but we still haven't won anything yet . . ."

Stallings and his team headed back to Tuscaloosa. They had one month to prepare for their Sugar Bowl matchup against Miami on New Year's Day in New Orleans. The winner would take home national championship rings to go with their Mardi Gras beads.

The Alabama and Miami teams couldn't have been more different. They both had winning records, but in terms of style and substance, the Tide and the Canes had virtually nothing in common. They were from two different cultures. Stallings had the Alabama team wearing suits and ties. The Miami guys? They were decked out in camouflage fatigues. The Alabama team was steeped in a Deep South, tradition-rich culture. Miami was proud but in a more modern and sometimes in-your-face kind of way.

As Alabama got off the airplane in Miami in their tidy, well-behaved row, the press was betting on trash-talking Miami. This served to fire up the underdog Bama players. And some retired players as well.

"When Lee Corso picked Miami, 21-0, over Alabama," remembered former star linebacker Barry Krauss, "that really ticked me off! I was like, we are going to beat their butts!"

Center Roger Shultz, who played in the late eighties and in 1990, also remembers Corso's comments. "He was saying, 'A high school team could beat Alabama.' That really gets you fired up!"

The 1992 team's defensive end, John Copeland, remembers seeing a sign when Alabama arrived in town: "13 and 0 and still ain't played nobody."

Jay Barker remembers reading a story in the paper that compared the upcoming game to a David and Goliath battle. "I don't know if they ever read the Word," Barker laughed. "But David won that battle."

The trash-talking and naysaying was serving to fire up the Bama squad. Most Bama fans didn't let the talk get under their skin—they knew better. Anyone who knew Gene Stallings knew better. You give Stallings a month to prepare for a ball game, and he's going to be ready. He's going to beat you! I remember longtime NFL coach Leeman Bennett saying, "Alabama's going to win." When asked why, he simply said, "I've seen the magic of 'Bebes' Stallings enough times to know. Trust me. Alabama's going to win." Leeman knew!

Factor in defensive coordinator Bill Oliver. They call him "Brother Oliver." Give him and Stallings a month to get ready and you can take it to the bank. They're going to win.

I felt sure of this because we had one of the absolute greatest defenses in the history of the university. In fact, it was arguably the greatest defense in the history of college football. The style was workmanlike and professional, substance over style.

These guys were not flashy. This was just an amazing bunch of players. Those who weren't that great in the beginning of the season became great later on because they had speed. They just rose to the occasion. Other guys on the team were just great ballplayers, period. Defensive ends Eric Curry and John Copeland, who both went on to the NFL, were the bookends on this team. You just didn't score on Alabama that year. The Tide allowed just 9.3 points per game in 1992.

Another thing working in Bama's favor was the fact that this team was remarkably healthy all year. Bama did not lose a single starter to injury for even one game during the '92 season. That's unheard of! Somebody's always getting hurt. But that year, the worst thing that happened to a guy was a hangnail. The same twenty-two that started the season opener against Vanderbilt started the Sugar Bowl against Miami.

Despite all this, as game time drew near Bama was still getting largely dismissed in the media. Only one writer, the *Tucson Citizen*'s Corky Simpson, voted Alabama No. 1. Despite the Tide's undefeated status, no one gave Alabama a hill of beans' chance to beat Miami because the Hurricanes had been dominating that entire year. Miami was the No. 1 team, and Alabama, as good as they were, still needed a couple of other teams to lose in order to move up in the ranks.

When we first arrived at the Superdome on game day, even Alabama's broadcast team got very little respect. The ABC guys, Keith Jackson and Bob Griese, had the big booth at the fifty. The legendary "Voice of the Philadelphia Phillies," Harry Kalas, who was doing the national radio broadcast, had a good-sized booth near midfield. The Miami network had a decent booth, too. Then there was us. Closer to Slidell than midfield. We got what was left over. It was as if the Alabama guys were an afterthought! The janitor's closet was bigger than our booth.

Once we found our closet, er, booth, we couldn't help but notice that there was a very large set of metal stairs bolted into the concrete riser right where we were supposed to sit. There was no way we could get all of our people in there with those stairs in the way. It had no bearing on one's size. We could have been the seven dwarves and we still would have had no room.

So, our spotter, Butch Owens, unscrewed the stairs and hauled them out to make room for everybody. The thing was though, now we had no stairs. We had to help our producer emeritus, Bert Bank, who was seventy-seven years old at the time, down this riser. Then I, not a small man, had to daintily climb down. (I believe this is the first time that the words *Eli* and *daintily* have ever been in the same sentence.) Plus we all had to file in, in order!

Bert went first, then our statistician Tom Roberts, then myself, Doug Layton, our color man at the time, and finally Butch. Once you got in, that was it! If somebody had to go to the bathroom, too bad! We couldn't leave. We couldn't move! When it finally came time to leave, we had to file out in order. It was right out of the *Three Stooges*!

But once you're on the air, the surroundings of the booth don't matter. The broadcast is the same. And this was one I'll never forget.

We were ready in our booth, and the players were readying for the kick-off. Eric Curry remembers the scene in the locker room: "Before the game, Miami was trash-talking right there on Bourbon Street," Curry said. "In the locker room, I knew something was stirring because usually Coach Stallings would bring us up and we would pray and go out there. But this time, Stallings stood up in the middle of the locker room and kind of looked around. It was totally quiet. He said, 'Alright guys.' And two at a time, we quietly walked out. I get choked up thinking about it. We were on!"

The players hit the field. Here came the kickoff and the Sugar Bowl was under way. On one of the very first plays, Miami's quarterback, Heisman Trophy winner Gino Torretta, looked up and saw all eleven men from Alabama's defense on the line of scrimmage, which was never done.

"We called it 'Eleven-Up,'" defensive back George Teague said, describing the unusual formation. "That meant everybody came up to the line of scrimmage. Coach Oliver put it in the game plan because you didn't see it much in college football then."

No Hurricane warnings tonight!

"Even offensively, we didn't know they were going to line up all eleven," remembered Jay Barker. "We didn't see that in practice. We were amazed at it as well."

Seeing the entire Bama defense lined up right in front of him was the beginning of Torretta's bad night.

Grand larceny by George Teague.

"In the second quarter, I saw Torretta look over at me and he froze for a second," said Bama defensive end John Copeland. "I saw fear."

For Torretta things just went downhill from there. As I remember it, the turning point in the game came after an incredible play that was ultimately called back on a penalty. It's known as, "The greatest play that never happened."

Torretta passed to Miami receiver Lamar Thomas, who made a fine catch after being left wide open when Tide cornerback Willie Gaston tripped and fell. Thomas took off running down the sidelines on his way to a touchdown when Alabama safety George Teague hightailed it after him and amazingly, caught up to him right around the Alabama fifteen yard line. The fans on both sides let out a collective gasp as Teague literally grabbed the football out of Thomas' arms! It was like he said, "Excuse me! I'll take that!"

Teague could have tackled Thomas or tried to force a fumble. But he went one better when he snatched the ball away, turned around, and ran the other way. He was soon taken down by an angry cluster of Miami players, but it was too late. The Alabama crowd was ecstatic.

Then, they saw the flag. Alabama had lined up offsides at the beginning of the play, so incredibly, this miraculous, one-of-a-kind display was called back. The thing was though, it didn't matter. Even though the play was nullified by penalty, it was another nail in the Miami coffin. They got the ball back but they knew they were beat.

Former Alabama defensive standout Bob Baumhower, who went on to an incredible career playing for the Miami Dolphins, remembers the scene in Miami before the game:

> Those University of Miami guys used to come down and watch the Dolphins practice," Baumhower said. "They were so cocky, as if we were supposed to be saying, 'Yes sir,' 'No sir,' to them! Then, watching that '92 defense line up, all eleven guys like that, saying, 'Hey, bring it on.' As a former Alabama football player I was so proud to watch that game.

Alabama won the game, 34-13, and took home the national championship. When they finished celebrating, Bama fans everywhere breathed a huge sigh of relief. After Coach Bryant passed away back in 1983, people wondered if it was the end of a great man's life and career, or was it the end of an era. The 1992 championship proved that even though thirteen years had passed since their last national crown, the tradition of winning national titles had not ended. This was very uplifting to loyal Bama fans.

Those of us who had crammed into the tiniest of broadcast booths felt beyond uplifted that night. We were sky high! The whole season had been a blast from the past, reminiscent of the glory days of the sixties and seventies. And now, to win the national championship was just magnificent.

The Superdome scoreboard framed by thousands of delirious Bama fans.

Of course fans back home were watching this tremendous event on TV. Barry Krause was one.

"I was sitting there, screaming and yelling!" he said. "My wife is from Indiana, and she didn't understand what I was going through. But when those guys on that team did that, all us former players were right with them."

I don't remember my feet hitting the ground as I began the very long walk from the New Orleans Superdome to the Hilton on the river, where we were staying. My wife, Claudette, was walking with me, along with our then-two-year-old daughter, Elise, and other broadcast crew members. That's a good mile or two, and I don't remember a minute of it except for the moment when I looked over, just before we hit the street, and saw Harry Kalas, walking along, carrying all his things in a shopping bag.

Harry is the longtime, incredibly beloved Voice of the Philadelphia Phillies. He was best known for baseball but also did football for CBS Radio. He became "the Voice" of NFL Films after the passing of the great John Facenda. He won the Ford Frick Award for his outstanding baseball broadcasting career in 2002. He's a hall of famer! I'd admired him for years.

Of all my non-game-related memories of this night, this image of Harry Kalas carrying this old paper shopping bag is the most vivid. There he was, schlepping his stuff. It just wasn't right. Did the handle of his briefcase break? I hope there was a good explanation.

"Now we've won something."

A few weeks later back in Tuscaloosa there was a huge celebration in Coleman Coliseum honoring this great championship team. I was the master of ceremonies for this huge party that was televised on closed-circuit TV. It went to alumni chapters everywhere and was viewed by Bama fans in far-flung corners of the globe. I remember saying, "I want to say hello to those of you watching in the Philippines!" The Million Dollar Band was playing. And there was a very special guest speaker: Corky Simpson, the Arizona sportswriter who had the distinction of being the only writer to vote Alabama No. 1 all year long in 1992.

Simpson perhaps felt a little shy about his honored guest status amid all the insane Crimson hoopla. He didn't brag about his foresight. He simply said, "Alabama just seemed like a good team to go with."

I think he sold himself short. I think he saw how awesome the defense was. I think he saw that quarterback Jay Barker, despite not being able to throw that long or run that fast, was a real winner. He saw that this team deserved to wear national championship rings for the rest of their lives.

God was definitely wearing a houndstooth hat in 1992. It was a magical year. Of course Coach Stallings had the last word. "Alright," he said. "Now we've won something."

TWENTY

Big Moments to Come

Looking at the Future through Crimson-Colored Glasses

So what's next for the Alabama Crimson Tide? As I see it, through my crimson-colored glasses, the future is as bright as its radiant past. True, because of scholarship limitations and the competition of the day, it's not likely that any team will totally dominate the college football landscape for years at a time like Bama did in the past. Yet among those few teams that will have a continual top-of-the-heap presence, Alabama is on the list. Why do I say this? On what can I base this optimism?

Well, simply put, there is history and tradition upon which to base my assessment. Every year will not be a national championship year, but, at the risk of sounding totally pompous, there will always be top-flight leadership at Alabama. There will never be a lack of coaching talent available because, record notwithstanding, there is a special cache to the Alabama Crimson Tide.

There is not a coach around who wouldn't jump at being the man in charge. A man to follow in the footsteps of the Wades, Thomases, Bryants, Stallingses and years from now when *he* chooses to retire, the Shulas of the world. And then most importantly, there will never be a lack of quality playing talent.

In our area of the country, many young men, from the earliest of ages, grow up wanting to pull that crimson and white jersey over their heads. Wearing that jersey makes them a part of the history of the sport.

Alabama. The name means sports history. Alabama. The name means championships. The Alabama Crimson Tide. Winners for life!

Looking back on seventeen years in the booth, it's hard to know where to even begin to talk about what the experience of broadcasting Alabama football games has meant to me. I have met so many incredible people and watched so many unbelievable games, they almost meld together.

As I write this, the Crimson Tide has just wrapped up its 2004 season, which ended with a tough Music City Bowl loss in Nashville to Minnesota that closed out a 6-6 season.

Bama is back in the bowl business at the 2004 Music City Bowl in Nashville.

Everyone—fans, players, coaches, team broadcasters—we're all feeling incredibly hopeful and upbeat. By season's end, the Tide had earned that bid to face the Golden Gophers in the Music City Bowl. This was great, great news. It had been a few years since Bama had played in a bowl game, and people don't even have to say out loud what this means: Bama is back.

The University of Alabama has made more postseason appearances (fifty-two) than any other college football team in history. Any other college football team! Anywhere! You just can't argue with a fact like that. There's no comparison to Alabama when it comes to bowls.

Bama's defense stops the Gophers for no gain.

Personally, I love traveling to bowl games. It's a terrific bonus for the players—many of whom may not have traveled to the host city before. And, as a broadcaster, I get to do what I love. Broadcast another Bama game! As long as I tag along with the Crimson Tide, I know where I'll be when the calendar flips over to the next year—at a bowl game.

IN 2003 THE UNIVERSITY OF ALABAMA HIRED MIKE SHULA TO BE ITS new head football coach. There were so many good things about this choice, but if I had to sum up all the good feelings in one word it would be *family*.

Head Coach Mike Shula.

Mike Shula is Alabama family. He is a Bama graduate who played quarterback from 1983 to 1986. He started his last three years and finished his career with a 32-15-1 record under coach Ray Perkins.

In his junior year Shula became only the second Bama quarterback to ever throw for more than two thousand yards in a single season. He may be best remembered for the thrilling win over Georgia in 1985. Bama was down, 16-13, with less than a minute remaining. Shula moved the team seventy-one yards in five plays and threw the winning touchdown pass. Put that on your résumé!

After graduation, Shula played for the Tampa Bay Bucs for two seasons, then went on to coach in the NFL for fifteen years, logging time in Miami, Chicago, and Tampa Bay.

Shula and his wife, Shari, have two young daughters and, of course, Mike's dad is a pretty well-known coach in his own right: the legendary Don Shula. What an ace up your sleeve to be able to call your dad, who also happens to be the winningest coach in NFL history, if you need to run an idea up the flagpole!

People had asked Mike Shula for years if he'd ever consider returning to Bama to coach, yet when he actually got the call to interview for the head coaching job, he said it took him somewhat by surprise.

"My heart started racing when I heard," Shula remembered. "At the time, I was living in Florida, where my wife and I grew up. We had friends and family there. I had a great job coaching quarterbacks for the Miami Dolphins. Was I ready to give all that up to go out and coach college football, which I'd never done? The answers to all these questions were yes, yes, and yes!"

There's nothing like running out onto the field at your alma mater as Mike Shula now knows.

Photo courtesy of Kent Gidley, the University of Alabama.

Shula interviewed on a Sunday, was offered the job on a Thursday, and flew to Tuscaloosa to meet the team that very night. He's only been back to Miami one time since. There was work to be done.

Ultimately, the history books will pass judgment on the coaching accomplishments of Mike Shula at Alabama. Clearly, as of this writing, in and around an unconscionable number of injuries, and in the aftermath of probation, things seem, to be heading in the right direction. A bowl appearance in 2004 was a sign of improvement. The successes of the 2005 recruiting season have also given Bama fans reason to smile.

When people make negative projections about a new coach, I love to tell them this: Think of the most successful coach or manager in the history of sports. Pick one. I don't care whether you name Vince Lombardi, Shug Jordan, Phil Jackson, Red Auerbach, Casey Stengel, hockey's Scotty Bowman, or Bear Bryant—pick anyone. Just remember, that guy coached his first game once. No one knew it was going to be the start of a dynasty. You've got to give the guy a chance.

When Shula arrived, there were scant few experienced players. The lingering effects of probation were there. Injuries seemed to come by the dozens to

Anthony Bryant (#97) haults a Kentucky drive.

Photo courtesy of the Paul W. Bryant Museum, the University of Alabama.

Bama's best frontline players. Yet, the team finished with a winning regular-season record in just his second year in charge. Very quickly, Mike Shula led the Crimson and White to a bowl game.

Next year, the inexperienced players will have experience. The probationary status will be another year further back and the injured will be up and running again with the excitement of what's to come. Trust me, Mike Shula's the right man to lead the Tide. He's a low-key guy with an excellent plan. He's got himself a ball club. A good one. And optimism abounds with good reason.

Coach Gene Stallings is among the many Bama optimists.

"I think next year's going to be a good one," Stallings said. "I've said a number of times it's going to take a while for Mike Shula to feel comfortable in this situation. But I think the people in Alabama want to see him be successful. The football team is in good hands. Mal Moore has done a good job as athletic director. They have just gorgeous facilities. The weight room, the dressing room. The way they've gone in and redone the areas for the players and coaches is going to be a real plus for them.

Bob Baumhower, the best purveyor of wings in Tuscaloosa, is yet another of the glass-half-full club: "I think Coach Shula is bringing back something very special," Baumhower said. "And that is pride, and a bond we have as ex-Alabama players that continues on."

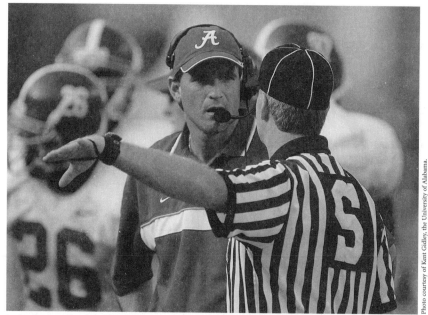

Laying the groundwork for Bama's future.

Photo courtesy of Kent Gidley, the University of Alabama.

For so many Alabama players, especially for those who are natives of the state, the pride had an early genesis. All-American John Hannah said the pride was instilled from the time he was a child. There was never any question where he would go to school.

"My dad said, 'You want to eat or not?'" Hannah said. "I wanted to eat. So I went to Alabama."

Kidding aside, Hannah said he brought two things with him from Alabama when he went on to become an all-Pro standout in the NFL.

"Class and pride," Hannah said. "That's what Coach Bryant taught. I think class is something you can't take away from any Alabama player. When I went to New England to play with the Patriots, I remember being interviewed for the first time. They asked, 'What's it going to be like playing in front of fifty-five thousand on national TV?' I told them I'd try not to be too disappointed. At Alabama, we were playing in front of eighty thousand to ninety thousand people!"

Major Ogilvie, who played running back for the Tide from 1977 to 1980, includes another word along with *class* and *pride—tradition.*

"It doesn't matter if it was this year or thirty years ago, going back to Coach Thomas or Coach Wade," Ogilve said. "What really separates the experience for us, as far as players at Alabama, is the tradition. The crimson jersey makes an impression on all of us and always has."

"I could never give back to Alabama what it has given me," former Bama quarterback Jay Barker said. "I could keep trying, but I'd never be able to pay it back."

I know the feeling. To take it a step further, picking the greatest moments in Alabama football history is an enormously daunting task. Whether we're talking about decades ago when Wallace Wade took Bama to its first Rose Bowl or Frank Thomas led a scrabbled-together squad of war vets and war babies into gridiron battle, where do you begin? We could talk about Bear Bryant for weeks. All his incredible accomplishments and the human story of a man who saw his players change over the decades. I mean, one of the man's biggest challenges was dealing with players who wanted to wear their hair long!

He changed with the times, begrudgingly agreeing to the long hair of the seventies if his players would agree to "Keep it clean for God's sake." He integrated the squad, installed the wishbone, inspired scores of players, and brought championship after championship home to Tuscaloosa.

When I think of my absolutely amazing experiences at Alabama, I think of Gene Stallings, a kind and dignified man who named his greatest accomplishment as the graduation of his players first and winning the national championship as second.

I think of the classic moments in our broadcast booth, for instance every time Joe Namath stops by to visit.

What could be better? Ken Stabler to my right and Joe Namath sitting to my left. I'm smart enough to know that when these two guys are in the booth with me, all I do is call the play and shut up. I just let those boys go!

There was one game against Auburn where Alabama was winning big. We were up, 31-7, at the time. We had a little break, when I asked Joe and Snake, "You know, guys, I can't imagine what it must feel like to be the world-class athletes that both of you guys are. When you do something on the field, 90 percent of the people will react either positively or negatively, whether they cheer you or 'boo' you. I'd love to know what that feels like! When you do something, everybody reacts."

"I know what you're talking about," Joe answered, "and sure, there is an adrenaline rush but you also pay the price. Look, my knees aren't great. I'm dealing with arthritis. Snake over here probably needs to get his knees replaced if not his hip replaced. I know why you would want that feeling, Eli, but there is a price to pay."

Then Snake jumps in. "You know what I want? I want Joe's little black book."

Joe says, "Well, Snake, it's not a little black book anymore."

"Why?" I asked.

Snake says, "I know why! You've used it so much you rubbed the covers off of it. That's why his knees are so bad!"

Great stuff. Just great radio.

I think of all the exciting games I've broadcast, like the 1989 matchup with Penn State in State College.

Alabama was undefeated that year. Penn State had lost only one game. The entire game was nip and tuck. Bama led, 17-16, but couldn't stop the great Penn State running back, Blair Thomas. The very last running play of the game for Penn State saw Thomas's knee hit the ground inside the Alabama one. It was very, very close to a touchdown. Literally inches to go.

So, Bama is up by a point, Penn State has the ball inside the one. Time is almost gone off the clock. They bring in their kicker, Ray Tarasi, who had already hit several field goals that day; one from forty-six yards out. This would be an easy one. Shorter than an extra point.

Well, we go to commercial and everyone in the booth is ticked off. Our sideline reporter back then was Jerry Duncan, a longtime Bama favorite, who usually came upstairs late in the game. He'd already come up and was sitting next to me. Our color man, Doug Layton, had already gone down to the locker room to prepare for his postgame interview with then head coach Bill Curry.

We thought it was over. So, here we sat with just seconds left. The vastly outnumbered Bama fans—there were ten thousand or so in the end zone—were silent. We were silent, just waiting for the eighty-five thousand Penn State fans to erupt.

But then a funny thing happened. The ball was snapped from the half yard line and we heard two thuds. The first was Tarasi's foot connecting with the ball, and the second was the ball hitting a body. Bama's Thomas Rayam just rose up like a Phoenix out of the ashes and swatted the football away. Game over. Bama wins!

Well, it was like someone threw a switch. Eighty-five thousand people stood up in stone cold silence. Then ten thousand people in the corner began cheering wildly.

Jerry Duncan starts yelling, "We blocked it! We blocked it!" He was jumping up and down and at one point, lost his footing and fell backward into my lap! He gave me a big hug and a kiss. And unless you're his wife, you don't want to be kissed by Jerry Duncan.

The emotion was unbelievable. I've never felt like that before. But I hope to, many times in the future.

True, I'm a broadcaster. But I'm also a fan. I would buy tickets to Alabama games if I weren't fortunate enough to have a seat high above the fifty yard line. There is just something about Alabama football.

"There's football in the South, then there's football in Alabama," Coach Shula said. "People are consumed by it year-round. Tuscaloosa transforms into something very special on football weeks. People start rolling in on Tuesday. It's incredible. There is nothing like it in the NFL or anywhere!"

Y'know, people always ask me about my job and I always say, I have the best job in the world. It's true. It really is. I have been blessed to have the opportunity to broadcast some of the biggest sporting events in the world. College football, NFL football, NASCAR racing, NHL hockey, baseball, CBS, NBC, ESPN. I have truly been blessed.

Over the years, my schedule has had to be massaged just a bit to make it all work. I have been offered some jobs that I have chosen to decline. Yet through it all, there has been one constant. Crimson Tide football.

I have turned down jobs because they would have interfered with my work with the Tide. I have had to negotiate with other employers to miss the occasional race or game, simply because I would not ever consider missing a Bama game. That was always a nonnegotiable point. You can't mess with my Bama games!

Being the "Voice" of the Crimson Tide is not a job, it's an honor. It is a position that is to be handled with care, like a precious piece of crystal. As the vocal conduit between America's most respected football program and its magnificent fan base, I have been fortunate to have the best seat in the house, from Tuscaloosa to New Orleans, from Miami to Honolulu. I sit in a seat from which I have been able to describe each and every minute of action while overflowing with Crimson Pride.

That's what this position means to me and that's what you, the Bama fans, mean to me. The Crimson Tide and Crimson Pride. ROLL TIDE!

Index

Numbers in *italic* indicate pages with photographs